ONLY YESTERDAY: *Collected Pieces*

Toronto's old Jewish neighbourhoods centered in the Ward and on Spadina Avenue are vividly recalled in these 18 evocative pieces by Ben Kayfetz and Stephen Speisman, both well-known chroniclers of Toronto's Jewish community.

Collected here for the first time are their colourful stories of the Jewish community and its daily concerns, synagogues and social institutions, Yiddish theatres and newspapers, and an assortment of memorable characters from Mayor Nathan Phillips to anarchist Emma Goldman.

Kayfetz is at his best as he explains the names of Toronto synagogues, as he does in an article from the *Globe and Mail* of 1955, or reminisces about the city's once-formidable Jewish press. He also provides a biographical sketch of the legendary J. B. Salsberg, remembers the Spadina Avenue and Kensington Market of yesteryear, and revisits the days when discrimination against minorities in home sales, hotels, department stores, private clubs and the professions was both legal and socially acceptable.

Speisman's articles include a masterful essay on the vanished downtown neighbourhood of St. John's Ward where thousands of Jewish families settled upon first arriving in the city of a century ago. He also sketches the history of the once-vibrant local Yiddish theatre and offers a profile of Benjamin Brown, Toronto's first Jewish architect who designed the Henry Street Synagogue, Balfour Building and other landmarks.

The text is enhanced with 144 photographs and illustrations, including dozens of photographs of former Toronto synagogues that have since been demolished or converted to other uses. Many were taken by Speisman and have not been published before. Additional photos came from the City of Toronto Archives, Ontario Jewish Archives, Archives of Ontario and various private collections.

"[*Editor*] Bill Gladstone has assembled some of the most memorable articles of key communal insider Ben Kayfetz, whose productive pen and keen eye combined to produce vignettes of everyday Jewish Toronto from the 1930s to the '50s. Gladstone has also unearthed many excellent articles by Stephen Speisman, premier historian of the community and a founder of its archives. This fine collection, prefaced by Gladstone's excellent introduction, will appeal both to everyone who wants to remember a city all but vanished through urban redevelopment and to historians of these exciting eras in Toronto Jewish history."— JACK LIPINSKY, PHD, author of *Imposing Their Will: an organizational history of Toronto Jews, 1933–1948.*

Ben Kayfetz, newsboy, age fifteen, June 1932.

ONLY YESTERDAY

Collected Pieces on the Jews of Toronto

by Benjamin Kayfetz and Stephen A. Speisman

With 144 photographs and illustrations

Now & Then Books

Toronto 2013

ISBN 978-0-9919009-0-9

The publisher would like to thank the Kayfetz and Speisman families for kindly extending permission to publish the articles in this book and for their enthusiastic support for this project.

The front cover shows a view from the steps of Toronto City Hall, looking south down Bay Street, ca 1925.

The back cover shows a view of Agnes and Teraulay (now Dundas and Bay) from an Eaton's building, looking northwest towards the Ontario Legislature, with the Teraulay Street Synagogue (Machzikei Hadas) in foreground and the Lyric Yiddish Theatre in a former church at centre right, Toronto, 1910.

Library and Archives Canada Cataloguing in Publication

Kayfetz, Benjamin, 1916-
    Only yesterday : collected pieces on the Jews of Toronto / by Benjamin Kayfetz and Stephen A. Speisman.

Includes bibliographical references and index.
ISBN 978-0-9919009-0-9

    1. Jews--Ontario--Toronto--History. I. Speisman, Stephen A., 1943- II. Title.

FC3097.9.J5 K39 2013   971.3'541004924   C2013-901670-8

NOW AND THEN BOOKS
www.nowandthenbookstoronto.com
Bill Gladstone, editor & publisher
www.billgladstone.ca

Contents

Editor's Foreword

THIS BOOK EXISTS because each of its authors had a passion for the history of the Jewish community of Toronto and for the city itself, a passion that I have shared ever since I began exploring my family's history half a lifetime ago. One of the best sources on the subject, Stephen Speisman's *The Jews of Toronto: A History to 1937* fascinated me and I read it until I wore out its pages. As my interest expanded I began to find obscure articles including various delightful pieces by Ben Kayfetz—for example his superb "Recollections of the Jewish Press in Toronto," which is a unique telling of a subject of which he had become intimately acquainted. His biographical portrait of J. B. Salsberg is likewise unexcelled; surprisingly, no one else to my knowledge has yet written of this important figure at such length. And I've yet to see another article like Kayfetz's "A Rabbinical Dynasty on Cecil Street" that recounts this particular chapter of Spadina-era history and lays it all out before the reader like a richly embroidered tapestry.

Speisman, it turns out, also wrote numerous masterful articles in addition to his valuable book. His "St. John's Shtetl: the Ward in 1911," for example, may be the best piece anyone has yet written about the Ward, that vanished, exotic neighbourhood that was so crowded with immigrants—Jews, Italians, Portuguese, Chinese—that it was commonly known as the city's "foreign quarter." He also wrote an excellent appreciation of Benjamin Brown, Toronto's first Jewish architect who designed many buildings of immense significance to the city. Similarly, Speisman's appraisal of "Yiddish Theatre in Toronto" is a welcome and fascinating foray into a subject about which little has been written.

Although their interests ranged over much of the same terrain, the two authors had vastly different approaches. Kayfetz's history is charming and informed, but somewhat idiosyncratic because he focused on what he thought was most interesting and didn't attempt to paint a comprehensive, balanced portrait. Superb at reminiscence, he is at his best when recounting his own impressions rather than when recanting stories from before his day such as those involving General Wolfe, the Harts and the Nordheimers. Speisman, by contrast, was a seasoned historian and careful scholar, as objective as Kayfetz was subjective. Their respective styles are a pleasing complement to each other.

Speisman's contribution to this book also includes dozens of photos from his large photograph collection, consisting of items he took himself (mostly in the late 1960s and early 1970s while researching his book) and a few items he acquired in that era from private sources. Kayfetz's informative article "How Were Toronto Synagogues Named?", which appeared originally in the *Globe and Mail* in 1955, seemed well suited to be illustrated with Speisman's photos of old synagogues and landsmanshaft buildings; as there are more such photos than the layout permitted, some are presented immediately following the article so as not to overwhelm the text. More are interspersed throughout the book.

The two Speisman photographs that I like best are both views of former synagogues from the Ward—Shomrei Shabbos on Chestnut Street and Shaarei Tzedek on Centre Avenue—with the New City Hall looming in the background. Who else was purposefully tracking around the old downtown neighbourhood, recording the last vestiges of the former Jewish presence in the Ward even as it was vanishing before our eyes? There is something poignant in seeing these disappearing relics of the old downtown juxtaposed with the most identifiable symbol of the new modern city.

The notion of an imperceptibly but steadily vanishing past is a key theme of this book and one reflected in the phrase "Only Yesterday," which crops up several times in Kayfetz's writings and so was chosen as the title.

From both a visual and textual standpoint, old synagogues are a key concern of this book since both authors focused a great deal of attention on them. As a result the book probably contains the largest assortment of photographs of old Toronto synagogues that has yet appeared in print. Although its treatment of the subject is not comprehensive, *Only Yesterday* could almost serve as a guidebook for anyone interested in downtown synagogues of the prewar era.

It must be noted that the Speisman photographs were not added to this project as an afterthought; indeed, they were the first element to be acquired. It took several years of cogitation for me to realize how wonderfully Kayfetz's written legacy would complement them, and vice versa. Only after arranging with the Kayfetz family for the rights to his scattered *oeuvre* did it dawn on me that Speisman's various uncollected writings would also fit perfectly into the mix. Additional photographs came from the City of Toronto Archives, the Ontario Jewish Archives, the Archives of Ontario, Library and Archives Canada, and various private collections including, of course, my own modest trove.

Regrettably, not all of Kayfetz's known pieces could be included in *Only Yesterday*. In particular, his reminiscences about growing up on Dundas Street and attending *cheder*—largely autobiographical pieces that conveyed more personal than communal information—had to be excluded for space reasons; sources for these pieces are included in the bibliography. With Speisman, the opposite was true: his pieces were few and far between. If only he had written more profiles like those on Benjamin Brown and Rabbi Meyer Levy! Avid readers are encouraged to seek out the various entries he contributed to the *Dictionary of Canadian Biography*.

People who "grew up Jewish" in Toronto will especially enjoy this book, as should anyone with a general interest in the history of the Jewish community or of Toronto itself. I hope the reader derives as much pleasure from reading *Only Yesterday* as I did in assembling its contents. I had the pleasure of speaking with Kayfetz on occasion and of consulting often with Speisman at the Ontario Jewish Archives. It is my fervent wish that *Only Yesterday: Collected Pieces on the Jews of Toronto* will bring both authors more of the recognition and attention that they so richly merit.

BILL GLADSTONE, *Editor & Publisher*

Pieces by Ben Kayfetz

Ben Kayfetz was born in Toronto in 1916. He trained as a teacher but, unable to get a teaching job in his native city because he was Jewish, taught briefly at schools in Niagara Falls and Huntsville. During his long and varied career at the Canadian Jewish Congress from 1947 to 1985, he fought for legal reforms to protect minority rights and was instrumental in establishing Ontario's Fair Employment Act, Fair Housing Act and Human Rights Code. A former president of the Canadian Jewish Historical Society, he authored *Toronto Jewry 60 Years Ago*, a pamphlet published by Congress, and wrote about Toronto's Jewish community for many publications including the *Globe and Mail*, the *Jewish Standard* and the *London Jewish Chronicle*. "He was considered by many to be a veritable walking archive and a wellspring of information on a range of historical and other subjects," the *Canadian Jewish News* wrote about him. "His open-door office at 150 Beverley Street was a place where politicians, community leaders and individuals with problems or those who just wanted to talk came to seek advice, exchange ideas or initiate projects." He was named a member of the Order of Canada in 1986 and died in Toronto in 2002.

Above, the only known photo of the People's Yiddish Theatre, Elm Street at University, ca 1908. It was the former home of Goel Tzedec Congregation from 1884 until 1906 when the congregation moved into the magnificent University Avenue Synagogue. Below, a TTC parade moves south along University towards Queen, ca 1911. The former synagogue and theatre, visible behind the two men in front, has been painted white.

This sketch, "Jewish Assembly Rooms, Richmond St. West," appeared in *Landmarks of Toronto*, ca 1897. The congregation may have been Chevrah Tehillim, the "Circle of the Psalm-Readers," a group that according to the city directory was situated above a blacksmith shop at 113 Richmond W. in 1896.

The Jews of Toronto—An Historical Sketch

THE FIRST JEWS to come to Canada were military men coming in the company of General Wolfe and his associates Generals Amherst and Murray. They settled in Three Rivers and Montreal and some of them, like the Harts of Three Rivers, became so well known that they were called the *seigneurs* of the area.

Jewish life in Upper Canada, however, started much later as did colonization in general on the Canadian side of the lower Great Lakes. Whether or not there were any Jews among the United Empire Loyalists who came to Canada has not yet been definitely established. We do know that there certainly were "Tories" (as they were known to the American revolutionaries) among the Jews of the American colonies and so it is not at all impossible that some of these may have migrated to King George III's dominions in what is

Published in pamphlet form by the Canadian Jewish Congress, November 1957, evidently to mark the centennial of Toronto Jewry. With additional material inserted as noted from "Toronto Jewry—Only Yesterday," Canadian Jewish Review, November 24, 1967. (1) indicates an added paragraph; (2) indicates an added sentence.

11

Left, Coombe's Drugstore, southeast corner Richmond & Yonge, 19th century. Sons of Israel (Holy Blossom) prayed in an upstairs room from 1856 to 1875. Right, Holy Blossom's first synagogue, Richmond Street at Victoria, was the first synagogue erected in Toronto; congregants faced south. The congregation sold it and moved to Bond Street in 1897. From *Landmarks of Toronto*.

now Ontario. It is possible that the diligent researcher may yet come across such data.

There are records of Jews settling in Upper Canada in the 'thirties and the 'forties of the nineteenth century. They came generally from two sources—an inner migration from the older established communities of Lower Canada or the occasional adventurers from the United States. In 1844 Abraham and Samuel Nordheimer, who had immigrated from Bavaria and had lived in Kingston where they were musical tutors for the governor's family, moved to Toronto when it became the seat of government. By 1846, records show that Toronto's Jewish population was twelve. There were, we have reason to believe, several attempts to form a permanent congregation in the city but these were unsuccessful either due to lack of members or inadequate organization.

There was one institution, however, that was too indispensable to overlook—a burial ground. In 1845 Judah Joseph and Abraham Nordheimer purchased a cemetery plot on Pape Avenue for a "Hebrew Congregation" that had not yet been established. This cemetery is still in existence today, a well-kept graveyard located in a populated working-class district in East Toronto and is a repository of much interesting data on our community's early days.

Historic plaque, mounted on building at the southeast corner of Richmond and Yonge Streets, marks the site of the first Jewish congregation in Ontario.

There is an early record of a communication being sent by the Upper Canada legislative council to the Mother Country enquiring if a Jewish house of worship may be exempted from taxation. The identity of this congregation and whether it was ever organized are questions that are still unanswered.

The Nordheimers, after whom the Nordheimer Ravine was named, came to Toronto in the 1840s; they were music teachers to the Governor's family and ran a company that manufactured pianos and sold musical instruments. One of the brothers, Abraham, returned to Germany where he died and the other, Samuel, was baptized an Anglican and married into the Family Compact segment of the city's upper crust. Even so, he always took occasion in public documents to mention his Jewish ancestry and continued to give to Jewish causes. The Nordheimers were connected through marriage to the Rossin brothers who in the 1850s built Toronto's fanciest hotel, the Rossin House (later the Prince George) at King and York Streets.[1]

By the 1850s, with Toronto growing and the railway era started, the city was ripe for a synagogue. The leading spirit was Lewis Samuel, father of Sigmund Samuel of today, a Yorkshire-born merchant who decided to settle in Toronto on the condition that there be a synagogue there. The story of the first meeting of the "Sons of Israel" and their first service in September 1856 in

13

a room over Coombe's drug store at Yonge and Richmond is by now a familiar one. Mr. Heinz Warschauer has told the story of the origin of the unique name "Holy Blossom" (no other synagogue in America has this name) and how the inscription of *Pirchei Kodesh* on the Torah pointer led to a search that ended in an English-language Jewish weekly in New York city. For the next thirty years the story of Toronto Jewry is identical with the story of the Holy Blossom Synagogue—then, of course, a traditionally Orthodox assembly. The "Jewish neighbourhood" still hugged the Richmond–York area. The first permanent structure of the Holy Blossom was on Richmond Street and Toronto's next two synagogues were likewise located on Richmond Street. In 1878 the first philanthropic society, the Ladies' Montefiore Benevolent Society, was founded, organized to dispense charity in the traditional Jewish manner.

Although Toronto Jewry is either 118 years old (if one estimates its age from the date of the Pape Avenue burial ground) or 111 years old (estimating from the first permanently organized congregation), its relative newness can be gauged by two facts: until only a few years ago Sigmund Samuel, son of the community's founder Lewis Samuel, was still among us; and Arthur Cohen, eighty-seven-year-old son of the Magistrate Jacob Cohen, still among us today, can recall his *cheder* days when the Holy Blossom was a wooden structure on Richmond Street in what is now virtually the pre-history of the community. The death a few years ago of Anne Franklin Robinson severed another link with the city's early Jewish community.[1]

The 1880s brought basic changes into the structure of Toronto's Jewish community. The pogroms of 1880 and 1881 which started the mass immigration from Russia to the United States left their mark on Canada as well. It was in the 1880s that the first permanent congregations of East European Jews were founded: the Goel Tzedec, the Chevrah Tehillim, and the Shomrei Shabbos. Some words of introduction may be needed about these congregations.

The Goel Tzedec is the oldest of the three. It was founded in 1883 on Richmond Street by Jacob Draimin, Abraham Cohen, Louis Levinsky, Nathan Smith and others. Its members were Jews

Southeast corner of York Street at Richmond, ca 1916. The "Jewish neighbourhood" hugged the Richmond–York area and the first premises of both Goel Tzedec and Chevrah Tehillim congregations were nearby.

from Russia, Poland and Galicia. Its home was a former church on Elm Street at University from 1884 to 1906, then the congregation moved into the magnificent, newly-built University Avenue Synagogue. In time Goel Tzedec became the senior of the traditional East European congregations, particularly after the Holy Blossom turned towards Reform. By the same token it was the first of these congregations (about 1920) to engage an English-speaking rabbi. It is rather interesting to note that the Goel Tzedec's engagement of an English-speaking rabbi took place about thirty years after the Holy Blossom's similar decision, this thirty years representing the approximate difference in age between the two.

The Beth Hamidrash Hagadol Chevrah Tehillim, to give it its full name, was organized in 1887 [as Chevrah Tehillim] at Richmond and York. Russian Jews dominated its membership and for a while in its early days it was jocularly entitled the *Kozatzky shul* (synagogue of the Cossacks). In 1905 it took over a Methodist church building on lower McCaul Street and from that time was generally known as the McCaul Street synagogue. In 1947 when Rabbi Reuben Slonim resumed his ministry there he restored the usage of the older name, keeping the first three words "Beth

15

Holy Blossom Synagogue on Bond Street, from The Toronto *Telegram*, ca 1920s. The inscription above the doorway contained the English name of the synagogue as well as the "Shema" prayer in both Hebrew and English.

Hamidrash Hagadol" or "the Great Synagogue." The McCaul Street synagogue vied in seniority for many years with the Goel Tzedec, being about equal in age and status. In 1947 it left the Orthodox fold and became affiliated with the Conservative wing of Judaism and in the 1950s fused with its friendly rival, Goel Tzedec, to form the new Beth Tzedec Congregation.

The Shomrei Shabbos from its outset was more of an "ethnic group" assembly than the other two which despite the domination of certain strains were not particularly identified with any "geographic" Jewry of East Europe. The Shomrei Shabbos on the other hand was always the Galicianer *kehillah* [community]. The family most closely identified with the founding of the congregation were the

16

Holy Blossom was the wealthiest and most assimilated congregation in the city and its rabbi spoke for the whole community. Although some East European Jews belonged, the Yiddish-speaking masses generally went elsewhere. Bond Street, interior looking towards rear, 1937.

Greismans. Although it was primarily an Austro-Galician shul, this did not mean that it was in any way isolated from the rest of the community, for we hear of its members constantly as participants in all-round Jewish communal activities. The unique feature of the Shomrei Shabbos is that it has remained today [1956] as it was seventy years ago—a traditional Orthodox congregation with strict partition between the sexes, sermons (or rather *droshes*) in Yiddish— and shows no sign of abating or diminishing its strict adherence to tradition. It has a flourishing daily *minyan* (at Brunswick and Sussex) of at least thirty people. Its rabbi is Gedaliah Felder who despite his youth is looked upon as an authority on *halakha* and Jewish law.

An interesting portrait of Toronto Jewry of that time is given in the Toronto *Mail and Empire* of October 1897. The article was part of the series entitled "Foreigners Who Live in Toronto" and its writer bore the pseudonym of "A REPORTER." According to the recent biography of Mackenzie King by Ferns and Ostry, this pseudonym was a cloak for the identity of none other than the young Mackenzie King who had recently graduated in political science at the University of Toronto and was serving an apprenticeship in journalism. The writer presents a picture of 2,500 Jews of whom

17

Rare photo of Holy Blossom interior on Bond Street, looking east towards the front. Note pipe organ and Hebrew inscription, *"Da Lifnei Me Atta Omed"*— "Know Before Whom You Stand." This is a poor reproduction from microfilm of a photograph that appeared in *Saturday Night* magazine, June 3, 1911.

three-fifths were Russian and Polish, the remainder German and English. He gives a well-balanced description of their economic status, trades and professions, their state of education and their religious devotion, giving details on *kashrut*, Sabbath observance, the Yiddish theatre, participation in trade unions, self-help, sobriety, and absence of criminal tendencies. He predicts that immigration would increase in the future. On the whole the article reveals a sympathetic but keen and intelligent observer at work, not surprising when we realize it comes from a young man destined to be prime minister of Canada for the longest period in its history.

By the late 1890s the more well-to-do and long-settled elements in the community had moved somewhat north to the Jarvis Street area which was then a street of fashion. It was in this period that the Holy Blossom Synagogue, often referred to as the "Toronto Hebrew Congregation," left its Richmond Street frame building and moved into a new building on Bond Street, constructed in Byzantine style, within easy distance of Jarvis, Wellesley and Church Streets. The building served the congregation for forty years until it was replaced in 1938 by the present edifice on Bathurst Street below Eglinton.

Mackenzie King described it as "an edifice which testifies more forcibly than words to the religious zeal of the Jewish people and to the place which they hold in the community today." He added:

"[W]hile it is unquestionably one of the finest structures in Toronto, it also is one of the very few of the many churches in the city which are without a cent of debt."

In 1897, the year which saw the dedication of the new synagogue, an event took place that was subsequently forgotten until it was unearthed recently by a staff member of the Canadian Jewish Congress. The Anglican Church had submitted a proposal for the introduction of Christian religious teachings into the public schools of Toronto. The Board of Education was inclined to accept it until it met with a vigorous three-thousand-word brief presented by the "Toronto Hebrew Congregation" (Holy Blossom) and signed by its rabbi the Reverend Mr. Lazarus, its president Alfred D. Benjamin, and its religious school supervisor Edmund Scheuer. The arguments and reasoning used in this brief are so cogent and so timely that they could be used in 1956 without changing a syllable. There are two rather outstanding facts about this event. First, that the tiny semi-"foreign" Jewish community of 1897, consisting to a great extent of raw and green immigrants with a leadership layer of persons with Western European or English education at its head, should be both bold and far-sighted enough to protest publicly and aggressively against this innovation which they saw as a threat to the democratic fabric and process. Second, that their protest succeeded.

The independent-minded, militantly dogmatic Protestant denominations of the day, particularly the Baptists, jealous of their doctrinal purity and wary of their children being contaminated by heretical High Church doctrines, joined in the Jewish protests. In view of this rally of public protest, the city solicitor discovered that there was no legal authorization for such teaching and the matter was shelved for almost fifty years to be reintroduced in 1945, successfully, by the provincial administration of the day.

While the founders of the Holy Blossom were for the most part Jews from England and Germany, there were from the very beginning Russian and Polish Jews within their ranks. The term "*deutsch*" as applied to the synagogue, just as it applied to clothing or

Shop operated by David Cohen (Kaganovich) at 164 York Street before the First World War was one of the earliest kosher butcher shops in the Ward.

literature, meant more than merely German. It also meant modern and "liberal" in the *haskalah* sense and could apply to customs and style of worship of Jews of whatever origin. Holy Blossom was popularly known as the "*deutschisher shul*" not because of any German origin—its founders were mainly English—but because of its style and outlook. Its posture of modernism was known to East European Jews as "German" long before Hitler gave the adjective other, more tragic connotations.[1]

After the turn of the century persecutions in Roumania brought large floods of Jewish *fusgeyers* who trekked hundreds of miles on foot across the Carpathian Mountains to the Austrian border town of Brody and beyond. Many came as refugees to Montreal and some continued on to Toronto where in 1902 they founded the Adath Israel First Roumanian Congregation on Centre Avenue in the Ward. It later moved to Bathurst Street near College and, in the recent era, to Wilson Avenue east of Bathurst, beside Highway 401. The kaleidoscopic ideologies which marked the Jewish Renaissance in Eastern Europe—Hebraism, the new Yiddish literature, Bundism, Territorialism, Zionism in all its various shadings—all these came with the stream of immigrants, a stream that was heightened

20

particularly in the time of the Russo-Japanese war of 1904 and the Russian revolution of the same year.

The area of first settlement of Toronto's East European Jews was the Ward—the district bounded by Bay Street, University Avenue, Queen Street and Gerrard—a segment of town they shared with the Italians, then a much smaller group than today. Within this area, later to be identified as Chinatown, were at least half a dozen synagogues. [1]

The decade and a half from 1900 to the beginning of World War One set the format of the multifaceted Jewish communal life that has remained to our day. Some of the new immigrants, interested in self-help and looking for security and familiarity in the midst of an uncertain economic existence and a new environment, banded together into sick benefit societies and *landsmanshaften*. Two of these, formed in 1905, were the Pride of Israel and the Mozirer Sick Benefit Society, and on their pattern there sprang up in the ensuing thirty years scores of such organizations, Toronto perhaps having more of them than any other comparable Jewish community on the continent. There are countless hamlets and *shtetlekh* of Eastern Europe particularly in Poland whose names have been commemorated in these associations, still quite active and faithful to their original purposes, contributing to all national and local Jewish causes over and above their sick benefit and insurance commitments to their own members.

The B'nai Zion fraternity—a brotherhood devoted to the ideals of the Basle programme—was started about 1903, only six years, we must remember, since Theodor Herzl had convened the first Zionist Congress. Two years later a group of idealistic individuals who were Zionists but at the same time shared certain socialist beliefs formed the first Poalei Zion unit in Toronto. These were the beginnings of a strong Zionist movement which from that point on was at the forefront of communal life in Toronto.

There was at that time an annoying problem that confronted the Jewish community: the question of the missionaries. The Jewish community had not yet developed its own welfare service resources to a point where it was able to adequately meet all the demands made upon it. A number of Jewish converts to Christianity sought to exploit the situation by making available the services of doctors, midwives and the distribution of direct relief in cases of childbirth, distress, unemployment, etcetera. In addition to these services there was an incessant street-corner proselytization in the Jewish district which, rather ineptly for its purpose, created more irritation than sympathy as the missionizing preachers would place themselves frequently in front of synagogues or rabbis' homes. On many a summer evening, folks out for a pleasant stroll in the Ward would be confronted by a "Jesus Saves" open-air address by the Reverends Henry Bregman or Morris Zeidman—both former Jews—delivered in Yiddish in a Talmudic sing-song.[2] To counteract this type of irritation the Folks Farein, an organization that gave assistance in the traditional Jewish manner, was formed in 1914. In 1908 the Hebrew Ladies Maternal Aid and Child Welfare Society was organized with Mrs. I. H. Siegel at its head. The following year the nucleus of an institution was set up at Elizabeth and Dundas that eventually became an orphanage and day-care centre for working mothers. In 1913 the Ezras Noshim was founded, a women's organization to look after sick mothers and help them with housework. It was from this nucleus that eventually were established the Mount Sinai Hospital and the Jewish Home for the Aged.

In 1911 Rabbi Solomon Jacobs of Holy Blossom delivered a sermon in the severe cathedral language of the day in which he scolded the Presbyterian church for its soul-snatching campaign, urging instead that it save the "fallen women" and the derelicts of its own faith and leave the Jews alone.[1]

In 1912 Toronto acquired its first local Jewish daily newspaper, the *Hebrew Journal*; until then the community had been served by American Yiddish dailies and the *Daily Eagle* of Montreal. Among the *Journal*'s editors have been such active communal workers as the late H. M. Kirshenbaum, the late Samuel Rhinewine and its present publisher, Shmuel Mayer Shapiro. The *Yiddishe Gass* of that day was the area from Teraulay (now Bay) Street west to McCaul,

The Folks Farein or Hebrew National Association, whose building on Cecil Street appears in this 1970 photo by Speisman, was founded before WWI to promote Jewish arts, but soon joined community efforts to counter the Christian missionaries. Its first headquarters was on Elm Street at Elizabeth.

from College south to Queen Street in "the Ward," that picturesque and colourful part of Toronto that has, apart from Chinatown, now been taken up by parking lots and hospitals.

Jewish education in that day was still to a great extent carried on in private *chederim* aside from the Sabbath School of the Holy Blossom which was conducted under the benevolent surveillance of the late Edmund Scheuer. In 1907 a Talmud Torah was established on Simcoe Street just below Dundas which in the first year had a registration of 100 pupils. Rabbi Jacob Gordon was the moving force behind its establishment. This was the ancestor of the present Associated Hebrew Schools system. What became known as the D'Arcy Street Talmud Torah, sponsored mainly by Polish Jews, was started some years later and at present too, has developed into a chain with three branches in the city. Its spiritual head for a while was the late Rabbi J. L. Graubart.

The years 1914 to 1920 saw an increasing tempo of development in Toronto's Jewish life. The community rallied early in the war for support of the war victims in Europe. A conference was called with Maurice Goldstick as its chairman and a group of volunteers went from door to door each Sunday collecting a "tax"

Headquarters of the Presbyterian Mission to the Jews, Elm Street at Elizabeth, 1913. These proselytizers provided medical services, relief and free meals to the Jewish community and especially children from poor families, often indoctrinating the children with Christian religious education at the same time.

for assistance for their overseas brethren. In the years 1916, 1917 and 1918, considerable soul-searching and debate went on about the feasibility and desirability of an all-Canadian Jewish organization for the service of Canadian Jews and to rally its efforts for fellow Jews overseas after the war and for what was hoped to be the establishment of a national homeland in Palestine. In Toronto as contrasted to Montreal there was very little opposition to this idea among the city's "uptown Jews" or from the Jewish press (which strongly favoured it, in fact).

In 1919, after considerable negotiation, balloting took place for elections to the Congress. It is interesting to see some of the names that appeared on that ballot or who attended the sessions, including many people still active in the life of our community today:

L. Bograd, Archie B. Bennett, Maurice Goldstick, Sam Kronick, Ben-Zion Hyman, J. Matenko, A. Kirzner, P. Shulman, Shmuel M. Shapiro, Dr. M. Pivnick, Sam Factor, S. Eisen.[1]

In 1920 under the impact of the postwar emergency the first Jewish overall campaign for overseas relief was conducted in which all elements of the community participated. Among the officers were Rabbi Brickner, Leo Frankel and Edmund Scheuer. Zionists, the Orthodox and Jews in general participated and the amount raised was in the neighbourhood of $100,000, a record sum for that day.

The period after World War One, going into the 1920s, saw another wave of immigration, this time primarily from Poland although there were a large number of immigrants from the Ukraine and Russia who came via Roumania. The 1920s also saw the settlement in Toronto, as in other Canadian cities, of war orphans from the Ukraine whose admission was secured through the efforts of Mrs. A. J. Freiman of Ottawa.

The Jewish neighbourhood by this time had moved in westward channels following the arteries of Dundas, College and Harbord Streets to Shaw and Dovercourt. By the 1930s there were offshoots in the Hillcrest–St. Clair area, but the great bulk of the population lived south of Bloor Street. The Spadina corridor, of course, was also crammed with Jewish life and vitality.[2]

It is not generally remembered that it was customary for Toronto's leading rabbis in the 1920s and into the 1930s to be associated with several synagogues rather than only one. The late Jacob Gordon was retained simultaneously by the Goel Tzedec, the McCaul Street Shul, the Anshei England and others. This did not imply necessarily that rabbis so retained received double or treble compensation. In fact, the stipends provided were so inadequate that spiritual leaders supplemented their income not only in the usual way of performing marriages, divorces, funerals, etcetera, but by engaging in business. The practice, incidentally, is not frowned on in Jewish tradition, which preferred that he not make a livelihood out of Torah.[1]

The Bond Street Synagogue had a knack for attracting bright young men to be rabbis in the 1920s—Brickner, Isserman,

Eisendrath—who inveighed against strapping in the schools and drew hundreds of Gentiles to their Sunday morning sermons. It was the congregation's home for forty years until 1937 when Holy Blossom built its present building on Bathurst and Ava Road. Today its former premises on Bond Street serves as a Greek Orthodox Church, a denomination for which its Byzantine domes are particularly appropriate.[1]

The 1930s with the Depression and the rise of Hitlerism in Germany brought new conflicts, questionings and stirrings into the community. Economic discrimination, exacerbated by a serious slump, raised the question of general economic security, and caused some questionings about the position of the Jew in the Diaspora. The menace of Fascism revived the Canadian Jewish Congress which reorganized in 1934 and which has remained a flourishing body since that time, giving leadership and assistance to the community. Events such as the swastika riots in Kew Beach caused concern and distress and made the Jewish ranks draw a little closer.

The story since 1939 is too recent and fresh in our minds to require repetition here. Toronto's Jewry's war effort, the personal sacrifices made and lives lost, the impact of the great European catastrophe on our lives as Canadians and as Jews, the establishment of the State of Israel and its effect on Diaspora life, its concerted and concentrated effort to assist Israel in its fight for life, the expansion of Toronto Jewry in numbers and its sharing of Toronto's increased prestige and influence—all these will be dealt with in better perspective no doubt in the sesquicentennial celebrations half a century from now, an event which our community can anticipate with some assurance in the light of the bright future expected for Toronto. ∝

The small congregation Chevrah Tehillim purchased a large Methodist Church on McCaul Street in 1905 and renamed itself Beit HaMidrash Hagadol Chevra Tehillim. That large name adorns the doorway in this 1920 view of the shul, popularly known as the McCaul Street Synagogue.

How Were Toronto Synagogues Named?

HAVE YOU EVER WONDERED about the meaning of those mysterious looking clusters of Hebrew letters inscribed over the doorways of Toronto's synagogues? Only rarely is an English translation provided side by side, for like so many names, they have acquired a personality and identity of their own to those who are on a basis of day-to-day familiarity with them, quite apart from their literal meaning. These names are an interesting study, a study which tells us something about the inspirations, the root sources, and the spiritual aspirations of those immigrants, mainly from

From the Globe and Mail, September 17, 1955.

27

Former home of Adath Israel, Bathurst north of College, 1966. The congregation was founded about 1900 by recent immigrants from Roumania. (Speisman)

Eastern Europe, who have established these houses of worship in the last sixty or seventy years.

The synagogue names fall naturally into various categories. There is first the most numerous category, the "ethnic" grouping, those synagogues founded by members who hailed from the same small town in Poland, Lithuania or the Ukraine, and who felt more comfortable worshipping together with men who pronounced Hebrew in the very same dialect they knew back home and who sang the familiar hymns in the cadence they knew as boys. Some are named after whole countries, like the Adath Israel Anshei Roumania on Bathurst Street at College Street (the flock of Israel of the Men of Roumania) established fifty-two years ago [ca 1903]. Today this synagogue is no longer a "Roumanian" congregation in any strict sense. Its rabbi is German-born and holds an MA from the University of Toronto. A few blocks away, on Augusta

D'Arcy Street church was former home of Anshei Shidlov, seen here in 1966, just one of dozens of "anshei" congregations that arose in Toronto. (Speisman)

Avenue, is another "Roumanian" synagogue in a renovated private dwelling, called the "Roumanian Congregation of Israel's Glory" and popularly known as the "Moldavian Shul," taking this name from the senior province of Roumania (*shul* being the Yiddish word for synagogue).

On the east side of Spadina Avenue, housed in a made-over church building, is the Hebrew Men of England Congregation— known popularly as the "Londoner Shul." Despite its name, the Men of England is not the synagogue attended by most British-born Jews in Toronto. Its original membership consisted mainly of Russian and Polish Jews who lived in the British Isles for some years before making their permanent home in Canada. In the case of some, their English sojourn was very little more than a three-week quarantine period in transit in London or Liverpool. However, the glow of English residence did not wear off and has remained with them to this day if only vicariously.

In the Beverley–Dundas–Spadina section there are clustered a concentration of these "Men of" congregations: Men of Shidlov, Men of Stashov, Men of Chmielnik, Men of Apt, Men of Ostrovtze,

Many of the "anshei" or "people of" congregations were from obscure villages or towns that few people could easily pinpoint on a map. Above, home of Anshei Drildz, 1966. (Speisman)

Men of Kielce. Most of these towns are located in Central Poland within about a 100-mile radius of Warsaw, and before the great Nazi annihilation were flourishing centres of traditional Jewish life and culture. The synagogue of Kielce, incidentally, is called in full: the Congregation of the Men of Kielce—Visitors of the Sick; the founders sought to incorporate in their name an old-established Jewish virtue as well as their place of origin.

Others scattered through Wards Four and Five South are called the Men of Slipia, Men of Narayev, Men of Drildz, the Men of Kiev. A tiny tabernacle on Euclid Avenue, which used to house an Italian Protestant sect, is called by the pretentious name of the "Holy Fellowship of the Company of the Community of Israel of the Men of Lagov."

On lower Huron Street, south of Dundas, is an obscure little house, the home of a forty-five-year-old congregation which, contrary to the general rule, takes its name not from a village in Eastern Europe but from America's greatest metropolis. It is called "Men of New York," its metropolitan name in striking contrast to its modest size. This name dates back to old pre-quota days more than thirty years ago when American immigration laws permitted

Anshei Lubavitch, Denison Avenue, as it appeared in 1966. In this case the name refers not to natives of the town but to adherents of the great rabbi who founded a new religious movement there in the late 1700s. (Speisman)

a totally unrestricted movement for all comers between the United States and other countries. In the same Spadina Avenue area is the Men of Minsk Congregation known popularly as the "St. Andrew Synagogue." How does a synagogue founded by Jews who stem from a White Russian provincial city come by this patronymic of a Scottish saint? Because it is located on St. Andrew Street and no one apparently sees any incongruity in calling it thus.

Sometimes the name "Men of" doesn't have the connotation of geographical origin. The "Palmerston Avenue Synagogue" is known officially as the Anshei S'fard—which is "Men of Spain." Not one of the members, however, can definitely trace his origin to the classical Hispanic Jewish golden age of Toledo, Seville or Cordova. In this case it means merely that the prayer book used in this congregation is patterned after the Spanish ritual. This divergence was initiated

Beis Yehudah Synagogue, Dovercourt Road, before its sale ca 1967. The congregation merged with Beth Emeth in Bathurst Manor in the 1960s. (Speisman)

in Eastern Europe by the rebellious sect of the Chassidim purely as a means of distinguishing their services from the conventional standardized worship prevalent in Eastern Europe. The "Men of Lubavitch" on Denison Avenue, south of Dundas Street, refers not to natives of the town mentioned, but to adherents of the great rabbi of that town who flourished from 1747 to 1812.

Frequently other phrases are woven in with these names. The synagogue of the Men of Drildz is the "Shelter of Righteousness of the Men of Drildz." Another congregation, recently moved from Augusta Avenue to Forest Hill Village, is the "Remnant of Israel of the Men of Lida."

A second favoured form of naming synagogues is the prefatory "House of." Eglinton Avenue's Beth Sholom (House of Peace) and Dovercourt Road's Beis Yehuda (House of Judah) are examples. (Beis is a variant pronunciation of Beth.) The House of Jacob on Henry Street is another (though this is more commonly known as the "Polish synagogue"). The Beth Tzedec—House of Righteousness— now nearing completion on Bathurst Street above St. Clair Avenue

Knesseth Israel, the Junction Shul, 1967. The synagogue was built on Maria Street soon after the congregation was founded in 1909. The shul's one and only spiritual leader was Rabbi Mordecai Langner, who served 1924 to 1939. (Speisman)

is a "composite" construction. Its name is a combination of the two congregations which merged about three years ago—the seventy-two-year-old Goel Tzedec (the Righteous Redeemer) and the sixty-eight-year-old Beth Hamidrash Hagadol Chevrah Tehillim (the Great House of Prayer of the Fellowship of the Psalms) on McCaul Street. Taking the key word from both names, the new name was coined.

Chevrah—"fellowship" or "company"—is a favourite nomenclature. Besides the "Fellowship of the Psalms" on McCaul Street we find on Cecil Street in an unassuming building a congregation called the Chevra Shass—the Fellowship of the Six Books. (So humble and unassuming was this congregation that it only recently hung out a sign, the members deeming a public placard as not in

Shaarei Tzedek, the Markham Street Shul, 1966. The name means "gates of justice" and the congregation consisted mainly of Russian as opposed to Polish Jewish immigrant families. (Speisman)

keeping with their state of piety.) The word *Shass* is made up of the initials of the Hebrew words *shisha s'farim*—six books. This then is a congregation named for (and which studies regularly) the six books of the Mishnah—the nucleus of the Talmud, compendium of Jewish law and lore. Half a block to the west is the Fellowship of Readers. On Markham Street above College is the Holy Fellowship of Brotherly Love.

A fourth style of naming is the prefix "Gates of." Thus on Markham and Ulster, the Gates of Righteousness (Shaarei Tzedek); on St. Clair Avenue, the Gates of Heaven (Shaarei Shomayim)—Toronto's largest and most modern Orthodox synagogue; and now under erection in the North York part of Bathurst Street, the Gates of Prayer (Shaarei T'fillah).

Two congregations are "Strengtheners" [*Machzikei*]. One on Dovercourt Road at Dundas is a congregation of "Strengtheners of the Children of Israel" and a new congregation (as yet without a building) in North York is "Strengtheners of the Faith."

In Toronto Junction, a remnant of the days when this was a separate municipality with its autonomous Jewish community, there still stands on Maria Street the "Assembly of Israel" (Knesseth

Shaarei Shomayim on St. Clair Avenue West, 1965, shortly before the congregation moved to Glencairn Avenue. Demolished in 2012. (Speisman)

Israel). In 1948 this was the name chosen for the Parliament of the new State of Israel. At the east side of mid-Toronto, in the old Cabbagetown on Berkeley Street (also a remnant of an earlier more populous Jewish settlement in the district) is the appropriately named B'nai Israel Hamizrachim—the "Eastern Children of Israel" congregation.

Other congregations spotted around the city show a wide variety in their names. On Shaw Street is the straight Biblical "Children of Israel"; on Brunswick Avenue and Sussex Street the sixty-eight-year-old "Guardians of the Sabbath" (Shomrei Shabbos) was founded on Chestnut Street as far back as 1888; a small congregation on Brunswick calls itself the "Voice of Jacob—Men of Truth"; another "the Complete Believers of Israel." Another "Learning and Labor" (Torah v'Avodah)—Americanized wags have called it TVA from its initial letters; a synagogue on College Street which is combined with a rabbinical seminary (yeshiva) is called "the Yeshiva of the Living Law" (Yeshiva Torat Chaim). A similar house of learning on D'Arcy Street is called the "Tree of Life" (Eitz Chaim).

The list is by no means exhausted. Nor is the reservoir of traditional names of congregations. If any kind of trend is discernible it is the tendency away from the "Men of" terminology. ❧

(Additional photos appear on next five pages.)

35

Voice of Jacob, Men of Truth — Kol Yakov Anshei Emeth, 1966. (Speisman)

Former home of Kielcer Shul, 450 Dundas Street West at Huron, 1966. (Speisman)

Anshei Lida—Congregation Shearith Israel Anshei Lida, 239 Augusta, ca 1954.

Fomer home of Anshei Slipia, 1966. (Speisman)

B'nai Israel HaMizrachim, the Berkeley Street Shul, seen here in the 1950s, served the pocket of Jews who lived in Toronto's east end. Even further east was the Beach Hebrew Institute, Kenilworth Avenue, founded 1920. (Speisman, 1966)

Semi-circular Hebrew sign—"Beit HaKnesset v'Talmud Torah d'B'nai Israel HaMizrachim"—once adorned the Berkeley Street Synagogue and later came to adorn this building on Parliament Street, possibly a Christian mission. (Speisman, 1971)

Anshei S'fard, the Palmerston Avenue Synagogue, 1966. (Speisman)

Congregation Machzikei B'nai Israel, 279 Dovercourt, ca 1966. Home of a Portuguese community centre in 2013. (Speisman)

Former Russian Shul, Shaarei Tzedek, on Centre Avenue in 1970, with City Hall and Sheraton Hotel in background. Storefront is later addition. The building, a remnant of the Ward, is long gone. See earlier views on pages 42 & 43. (Speisman)

Toronto Jewry, Only Yesterday

As THE YEARS RUSH BY in their unstoppable passage, the relics and artifacts of Toronto's Jewish story seem fewer and fewer.

Until some twenty years ago there were still several rag depots and abandoned warehouses in the old Ward section of Centre Avenue and Chestnut Street in whose outline could be recognized the structures of former synagogues. Near the corner of Elizabeth and Elm could be discerned the outline of a structure that once was an early home of the Poilisher Shul (now the Beth Jacob v'Anshe Drildz on Wilmington and Overbrook in suburban Downsview). Directly across was a regalia company manufacturing special buttons, tags and uniform accessories. The previous occupant, I recall, was the head office of the Presbyterian Church of Canada which originally had located on this corner in the heart of the Ward to preach its missionary message to the Jews who lived roundabout.

It was this enterprising mission that provoked Rabbi Solomon Jacobs of Holy Blossom Synagogue to invoke his fiery denunciatory

From a typed manuscript, 1984.

Shaarei Tzedek, Russian Shul, Centre Avenue, ca 1900–10. This
photo was the key to identifying the same building on next page.

sermon of 1911 that was reported extensively in Toronto's daily
newspapers. Said Rabbi Jacobs: ". . . If it were used to reclaim
drunkards, wife-beaters, fallen women, idle loafers, street roughs
and the Godless element who walk about the city using vile
and blasphemous language . . . and if funds are still left, let the
Presbyterian Church form a society for the conversion of so-called
Christians to the true teachings of Christianity as it was taught by
the Founder of the faith."

One persistent and surviving landmark that links 1984 with the

This 1917 photo was taken to document municipal street cleaning on Centre Avenue. As is clearly evident from photo on page 42, the building at right is Shaarei Tzedek. Building at left may have been a Christian Mission to the Jews.

very earliest date in Toronto's Jewish history is one that many of us pass by every day without giving it a second thought. On Spadina Avenue one block south of Dundas Street stands a factory building, the ground floor of which is given up to Chinese retailers. Spread across the length of the building is a large quite readable sign— Henry Davis & Co., Limited.

Henry Davis was born across the lake in Buffalo, New York, in 1854. Despite his birth in the United States his family was already part of the Canadian stream. His father Isaac Davis is described by historian B. G. Sack as the first Russian Jew to settle in Toronto. He had come to Canada in the 1830s and was already a Canadian citizen in 1837, the year of the Rebellion in Upper and Lower Canada, probably the first Jew from Eastern Europe to be naturalized. He lived in Montreal, in Quebec City and for a brief period in Buffalo before settling in Toronto in the year of his son's birth.

We knew that Henry attended public school in downtown Toronto (on Louisa Street) and went to Jarvis Collegiate. Henry married a girl from London, England where he resided for some years. He established a woollen manufacturing business and was actively involved in Jewish communal and synagogue life, being described as "strictly Orthodox" in religious views but very broadminded.

His youngest son, Bertram, administered the business after

43

Former Shomrei Shabbos Synagogue, 109 Chestnut Street, with rear of Toronto City Hall in background, 1966; the building then housed the Central Bag and Burlap factory. For view of Shomrei Shabbos ca 1900, see page 179. (Speisman)

Henry Davis's death in 1914 and this writer recalls seeing an obituary notice on Bertram some ten or fifteen years ago. Here we have more than 150 years of Jewish history in Canada and Toronto contained in that old factory building on Spadina Avenue and Grange. How many who pass it on foot or by vehicle pause to consider this? How many know it? The fact is: the vast majority, whether Jewish or Gentile, are totally unaware of this link with history.

On Pape Avenue at Gerrard Street in the midst of what is now a Chinese and East Indian neighbourhood stands the original cemetery of the Toronto Hebrew Congregation, the charter of which was obtained in 1849 from that stalwart of the Family Compact, John Beverley Robinson (from whom are named in turn Beverley Street, John Street and Robinson Street—all three former thoroughfares of Jewish residence and activity). The group which obtained the charter, researchers say, was not a synagogue entity called together for daily or weekly *davening* but a group of individuals who were concerned about proper burial of the dead, an important obligation in the roster of Jewish duties.

44

Shomrei Shabbos moved to this building at 225 Brunswick
Avenue in 1933. Speisman snapped the photo in 1965.

Seven years later, on Rosh Hashana 1856, a prayer group was
established over a drug store at Richmond Street and Yonge, calling
itself the Sons of Israel. By the 1860s the burial society and the
prayer *minyan* had merged. The corporate name taken on was that
of the burial society, Toronto Hebrew Congregation, which to this
day is the name on cheques issued by the institution. The name
Sons of Israel fell by the wayside and was eventually replaced by
Holy Blossom. Where that name came from is quite another story
and requires a separate account.

The denseness and ubiquity of Jewish institutions in the Bathurst–
College–University–Queen quadrant as it was up to the end of the
1950s reflected the economic and the cultural physiognomy of the
Jewish community of that day; evidence of our former presence is
disappearing but the stories endure. People lived fairly close to their
workplace back then: who had cars? Earlier, when the immigrants
worked at Eaton's sewing manufactories, the homes were huddled
close by on streets running off Bay (then Teraulay) up to Gerrard
Street. When the garment district moved to Lower Spadina, the
Jewish immigrant population shifted to the streets running east
and west from Spadina Avenue as far as Bloor Street where they
were blocked by the more expensive real estate of the Annex. (A
number of Jewish *g'veerim* were, of course, Annex dwellers residing
in dignified dwellings along Madison Avenue, Huron Street and
Lowther Avenue.)

And all the support institutions—the synagogues, the *lands-*

45

Congregants on steps of Hebrew Men of England (Londoner) Synagogue, 1933. Few if any were actually from London or England.

manshaften, the mutual benefit associations—were also quite close by the synagogues because members, being pious, had to be within walking distance.

The names of the institutions read like a gazetteer of Eastern European *shtetlekh*: the Anshei Chmielnik (on Huron Street and later on Winona Drive), the Anshei Kielce, the Anshei Minsk (not to be confused with the Minsker Farband), the Ostrovtzer Shul (and its secular counterpart the Ostrovtzer Farband several blocks distant), the Zaglembier Society, the Wierbzniker Farein, the Shearith Israel Anshei Lida Synagogue, the Anshei Drildz (separate from the Drildzer Young Men), two Roumanian congregations—the Adath Israel Anshei Roumania which first arose on Chestnut Street, and the Moldavian shul on Augusta Avenue; the Stashover shul and the separate Stashover Young Men; the Anshei Slipia—the list is endless.

Some of the above-mentioned societies included the descriptive phrase "Young Men," and there is little question that at the time of incorporation their membership consisted of the youthful element. But as the decades rolled by they could no longer with any semblance of justice or voracity be termed "Young Men." But just as sickly babies were named *Alter* (old one) to deceive the angel of death, the reverse was applied to the young men, now grown old, in the hope

46

A fire, started by natural causes, ravaged Hebrew Men of England Synagogue, east side of Spadina Avenue, July 1960. It was not rebuilt. (Speisman Collection)

perhaps that *nomen est omen* and the aging process could be halted. And some synagogues disdained the plebeian parochialism of a *shtetl* nomenclature: they had higher claims to a more impressive and sophisticated provenance.

On mid-Spadina, dominating that broad thoroughfare stood the Anshei England, known commonly as the Londoner Shul. Why London and England? Were these the Samuels and the Benjamins who had earlier been associated with the Holy Blossom? The fact is they were in the main the same Russian and Polish Jews as all the other arrivals. But some had spent a period, however brief, in Queen Victoria's blessed realm and the Anglo-Jewish lifestyle and flavour had appealed to them, accounting for the anglophile title. At one point in the 1960s there was a communication sent to the Board of Deputies of British Jews in London, in the heart of Empire, to broach the matter of a direct affiliation with the Board, but nothing seems to have come of it.

The other "metropolitan" name was based on the second "world city"—New York. The Anshei New York, however, made no pretense of being a major house of worship. It was a lowly *shtiebl* on a side street south of Dundas. There was a distinct discrepancy between its high-falutin name and its modest locale. Its members were in the main humble needle workers—which is the key to the origin of the

Hebrew Men of England's new building on Bathurst Street at Canyon Road, ca 1972. The congregation merged with Beth Emeth in 1975 and the building was torn down. (Speisman)

name. Prior to the imposition of the US quota laws there was free and unimpeded movement across the American-Canadian border. As the seasons shifted the migrant needle workers travelled between Toronto's garment district and New York's Seventh Avenue. But when the gates were closed shut in 1923–24 those who chose to stay in Canada (or had no alternative) had at least their memories of those days of free exchange between the nations and put those memories into the proud name "Anshei New York."

Oddly enough, both "big city" establishments have not lasted. The Londoner moved up north but eventually gave up the ghost. What became of the Manhattan conventicle since its Huron Street days is not known to this writer.

Twenty-four Cecil Street was the address of the Labour Zionist movement and its Farband Folk School up until about 1950. Today, ironically, it is the headquarters of a political party which Labour Zionism consistently opposed—the Communist Party. After a recent fire it was rebuilt to the exact specifications of the earlier original building. A block away, where the late David Shatz ran a permanent non-floating chess game, was a centre that housed the General Zionists and Young Judea. It was demolished some years ago and its replacement now houses the Polish Veterans. Around the corner on Beverley Street stood a building that was the Peretz School and the meeting place of the Arbeiter Ring, a non-Zionist socialist fraternal order known in English as the Workmen's Circle. A year ago, it too was demolished to make way for an enlarged centre for the mentally retarded.

48

These centres—and institutions like the Labour Lyceum and the Standard Theatre—were at the heart of Toronto's Jewish cultural life in the immigrant period which was vigorous and full of pith and substance.

Religiously, the community was divided along internal ethnic lines rather than gradations of piety, for all subscribed to the same level of piety. The Galician Jews regarded Rabbi Joseph Weinreb as their spiritual head. This by no means indicates a unity in their ranks for they fought bitterly internally on other matters. The Toronto daily newspapers carried an account of a donnybrook that broke out in the Shomrei Shabbos Synagogue in Passover 1906 when not only fisticuffs took place but bloodthirsty shouts of *"m'shnajt helzer un brakht bajner"* (*"cut throats and break bones"*) went hurling in the air. (The eyewitness source for this, supplementing the contemporary press report, is lawyer Henry Papernick, then an eight-year-old boy).

The *mara d'atra* of the Jews who came from Russian Poland was at first Rabbi Yudl Rosenberg, a noted scholar (he is the grandfather that Mordecai Richler refers to in his earlier novels). A few years after Yudl Rosenberg moved to Montreal he was succeeded by another scholar, Yehuda Leib Graubart, who produced a sizeable number of disciples in his nineteen years in Toronto before he died in 1939.

The Russian and Lithuanian Jews paid allegiance to Rabbi Jacob Gordon, a mild-mannered man who was one of the founders of that educational complex now known as the Associated Hebrew Schools. It started in an unimposing building on Simcoe Street in 1908. Toronto was not free, however, of rabbinic squabbles, *kashrut* quarrels and internal disputes—all of which are well covered in Stephen Speisman's well-known study, *The Jews of Toronto: A History to 1937*. While the community (or communities) paid ample respect to these rabbis they did not necessarily maintain them adequately or provide a living salary. Most had to supplement their income, some by real estate dealing or various other means. Some were agents for kosher wine firms.

Even their salaries from synagogues were uncertain and vague.

Yakov Kamensky (bearded) with students of Yeshiva Maril Graubart ca 1943, four years after death of Y. L. Graubart (inset). From Eitz Chaim's 25th anniversary book, 1943.

A revealing light was thrown on the income of rabbis when in 1932 several were cross-examined during a dispute about *kashrut* jurisdiction that reached the Gentile courts. Rabbi A., one of the leading rabbis, was asked: Did you receive $1,500 a year in salary from the Congregation? The answer, given laconically by the rabbi: "They say I receive."

How does the Jewish community of the 1980s differ from the earlier community of the 1920s and 1930s? Generalization is difficult for what is sometimes seen as a trend may later be belied by a divergent and contradictory trend. In one respect we are a more nativized and cultivated community. To the disappointment and dismay of some, English has displaced Yiddish as the common tongue of the institutions, be they fraternal orders or synagogues.

The distinctions (cultural, geographic, economic) that had existed between the longer-settled elements and the newer immigrants, *i.e.*, post-World War One, have long been eroded. Does this sound as though Toronto Jewry is now a monolith, a monochrome community of White Anglo-Saxon Hebrews (washes) with the colour and exotic qualities of a former generation thinned out beyond recognition?

Far from it.

Toronto's Jewry is far more diverse than it ever was. In the 1920s

Yeshiva Maril Graubart,
80 D'Arcy Street, 1966. (Speisman)

and 1930s we were all East European and the only distinctions (which for the most part were held mock-seriously) were the difference between sweetened and peppered gefilte fish, the jarring outlandish diphthongs of the Galicianer and the sibilant hiss of the Litvak (the adjectives are supplied subjectively depending upon the listener's own Jewish ethnicity).

Late in the 1930s came a handful of German, Austrian and Czech refugees (we know now why it was only a handful, thanks to the research of Professors Abella and Troper). From 1947–48, came a new infusion of Polish and Baltic Jews from the Displaced Persons camps. After the Hungarian uprising of 1956 came a contingent of Hungarians who, though Ashkenazim like the rest, had acquired the Magyar language which set them apart from the earlier arrivals.

But starting in the late 1950s came a totally novel element stemming from an older branch of Jewry and a senior tradition that had persisted while living for centuries in quite a different social and cultural milieu—the Sephardic Jews of North Africa, more particularly those of Morocco. These in turn were divided between the francophones of former French Morocco and the hispanophones (to coin a word) of Tangiers and former Spanish Morocco.

Finally—the Russians. These are drastically removed in every way from the Russian Jews who came in earlier eras. Those were from the *shtetlekh* in the Pale, their language was Yiddish, they were indelibly and incurably Jewish, and their expectations and aspirations were little different from the Jews from other parts of Eastern Europe. The Russians who came in the 1970s and 1980s are people who had been subjected in many cases to sixty years of overpowering and all-consuming pressures of the totalitarian Soviet State. They are not from the *shtetl*, they are from the large cities—Dniepropetrovsk, Kiev, Leningrad, Moscow. Their Jewishness is minimal, coming from a land devoid of Jewish schools where Jewish religious education was forbidden (and Jewish secular education in effect banned) and where synagogue attendance and membership were certainly not encouraged. The entire process of reclaiming these for Jewish posterity, present and future, is on the communal agenda in many different ways.

In former days Chassidism was a plant that did not travel well. There was the Strettener Rebbe on Cecil and Huron Streets whose get-togethers were well frequented communal events; many of these visitors, however, were curiosity seekers. He had a limited number of disciples confined, mostly to those of Galician provenance. Today one can go to the Lubavitcher and the Bobover to mention two Chassidic groups and one finds third- and fourth-generation Canadians stemming from Liberal, Conservative and "indifferent" families who have adopted the Chassidic approach and lifestyle.

So for every generalization an exception is provided. Assimilation and intermarriage seem to be on the rise but simultaneously more intense and more traditional forms of Jewish expression are proliferating here. Such trends were unknown earlier. Membership in Zionist youth groups is down but interest in Israel among youth seems unabated. There are far more of us who are Canadian-born than are shown in the 1931 census, but there are now among us Jews from India (both Bene Israel and Baghdadi), from Iraq, from South Africa and the USSR, as well as reinforcements from post-war Poland and surviving pockets in East Europe.

Ad for "Her Mother's Wedding Gown," at Standard Theatre, 1928

Recollections of the Jewish Press in Toronto

MY REMARKS ON THE JEWISH PRESS in Toronto must not be mistaken for any kind of definitive study. They are only my highly subjective, very personal, very imperfectly recalled observations based on my exposure to the Jewish periodicals of the city since childhood, going back some fifty-five years.

My first experience was with *Der Yidisher Zhurnal*, which carried the English name the *Hebrew Journal* even though it was written in Yiddish not in Hebrew. Possibly, back in 1913 when the paper was established, the feeling was still prevalent in certain circles that "Jewish" was too stark a word, and "Hebrew" more refined. It appeared six days a week, every day but Saturday, and met the needs

Presented to the Canadian Jewish Historical Society, Ottawa, June 1982. An abridged version appeared in Polyphony: Journal of the Multicultural History Society of Ontario, Summer 1984, and in The Rise of the Toronto Jewish Community, by Shmuel M. Shapiro (Now and Then Books, 2011).

53

of the immigrant population for five decades. In my own case, at *cheder* my Hebrew teacher spent a few minutes with me every day going over the *"Neies Bei Unz in Shtot"* section of the paper, which was a summation of the local general news—a story involving a Jewish pedlar who was arrested, a theft here, a violent robbery or hold-up there—all culled from the metropolitan downtown press. This daily review gave me a personal intimacy with the Yiddish press which has never left me to this day.

Throughout its history the *Hebrew Journal* had to withstand stiff competition from the three (and earlier four) Yiddish New York dailies, which were on sale in Toronto on the same day they were published. There was a joke that circulated in the city—it was similarly told in New York about the *Tog* and *Forverts*—"How did the *Toronto Star* find out a full day in advance what news reports the *Journal* would publish the next day?" In New York it was the *Times* in place of the *Star*, but the implication of "scissors and paste" and quick translation was the same.

It is probable that when the *Forverts, Morgen Zhurnal, Tageblatt* and *Tog*, all of New York, were publishing, their combined circulation in Toronto was far greater than that of the *Journal*. This sort of competition is something the *Globe*, the *Telegram* and the *Star* never had to endure. Yet the amazing thing is that the *Journal* survived as long as it did into the 1960s. It lasted twenty years longer than similar Yiddish dailies in American cities with much larger Jewish populations—Chicago, Cincinnati, Boston, Philadelphia and Cleveland—whose daily local Yiddish papers expired in the early 1940s. For the most part, in the 1950s there were no Yiddish dailies anywhere in the United States outside of New York City; while in Canada, the *Keneder Adler* in Montreal and the *Hebrew Journal* in Toronto were still appearing six days a week.

How the *Journal* managed was a mystery that only its longtime editor and publisher, Shmuel Mayer Shapiro, knew the answer to. What kind of person was Shapiro? He was a virile looking individual of leonine appearance with a luxurious mane of hair that had only begun to show a few gray strands after he turned seventy.

Mastheads of the two leading Yiddish newspapers in Canada. Top, "Der Yidisher Zhurnal"—the Daily Hebrew Journal of Toronto, 1928; bottom, "Keneder Adler"—the Canadian Eagle of Montreal, 1944.

He was from Mozir in White Russia and therefore a Litvak which put him into a minority position in Toronto where the preponderant majority of Jews were from Poland. But this never diminished him in his influence or his activity. Like the proverbial Litvak he was a skeptic; moreover, he was a hard-boiled cynic. As the editor of a *klal Yisroel* newspaper he managed to be all things to all people: he was a card-carrying Conservative and also an active proponent of the Histadrut and the trade union movement in Israel and therefore close to Labour Zionism. Being a Tory never stopped him from supporting Liberal candidates for office though one of his permanent proteges was Nathan Phillips all through the latter's thirty-year aldermanic career. Shapiro had a black list of persons and agencies who never were to be mentioned in the columns of the paper. What these were I never knew, though I was told of the list by an associate.

Shapiro had a group of "angels" he would turn to when the paper needed an infusion of money or when the creditors were getting impatient. Among the backers were Ben Sadowski of Toronto, Sam Bronfman of Montreal, and Melech Grafstein of London, Ontario who was the landlord of the paper's premises at 542 Dundas Street West in Toronto. Those of you who remember Max Grafstein recall

Nachman Shemen (left), ca 1930s; Abraham Rhinewine ca 1920s; Dorothy and Henry Dworkin and daughter, Toronto ca 1915.

him as an eccentric but successful businessman who saw himself as a publisher, a patron (a *metzenat* or *shtitzer,* as it's called) of the Jewish arts, of literature, the drama and publishing and culture *biklal* (generally). But Grafstein withdrew his patronage in a dispute about editorial control. Within a few months Shapiro and the paper moved to new quarters at College and Lippincott Avenue where the paper remained for approximately ten years.

The exchanges in the *Journal* were often fierce and many talented writers contributed. Both editorial views and styles were highly personal. For example, when Shapiro, under a pseudonym, referred to one of his backers and contributing writers as a *graphoman,* their collaboration ended for good. In the world of Yiddish writing there is nothing more offensive than being called a *graphoman.* It is a bit of a surprise that this useful expression of Greek origin has not entered the English language. A *graphoman* is someone who suffers from the disease of graphomania, an extreme obsession with writing without the commensurate and required talent that should accompany it.

Shapiro was a consummate cynic though there were certain causes he was not cynical about, such as the Histadrut and the Congress. He was one of those who, like Archie Bennett (whom he called *Ahr-tche* Bennett, as was the correct Yiddish diminutive

56

Youthful photo of Rose Miller, later Dunkelman, prominent philanthropist, Zionist and founder of the Jewish Standard, Toronto ca 1905. Right, Shmuel Mayer Shapiro, longtime editor and publisher of the Hebrew Journal, ca 1930s.

of Aharon), were believers in the ideology of Congress, that Congress was the soul of the Jewish "masses," that only it could keep together the integrity of the Jewish people. One group in Jewish life for whom he made no secret of his dislike were the Agudists. In fact there was one distinguished rabbi in the city whose affiliation with the Agudas Israel I was unaware of until I heard Shapiro denounce him once as an *Agudah'nik* (note the derogatory suffix).

Shapiro once commissioned my colleague Nachman Shemen (before he was my colleague) to do a history of the Orthodox Jewish community in Toronto which Shemen completed after considerable research. A fund-raising dinner was held but because the money raised didn't measure up to expectations Shapiro scullied the entire project even though the special supplement had already been printed. The copies were stashed in a cellar somewhere, they were never circulated and eventually were lost. Fortunately Mr. Shemen retained a copy and the text wasn't lost to posterity.

Shapiro gathered around him a number of writers of talent and ability. Most of these writers had been Hebrew teachers previously and some still doubled as such while they were employed as writers. There was Moishe Fogel who had a column in the paper each day and S. A. Abella who would send in reports on

Ad for Abraham Rhinewine's Yiddish book, "Der Yid in Kanada," published 1925–27. Hebrew Journal, 1928.

the Hapoel Hamizrachi movement. There was Itzchok Feigelman who wrote feuilletons in the European manner, sometimes using the understandable pseudonym of Tzippori. Nachman Shemen also wrote under his own name and various *noms de plume* such as Nachmani, N. Boimel, Ben Zalman. This, by the way, must be one of the few cases where a writer's original name becomes one of his pseudonyms. In later years there were Bernard Wind and Jacob Beller, both incidentally Galicianer. (Beller would bitterly complain to me of Shapiro, and though Shapiro tended to play the autocrat, I could never judge who was right). I still [in 1982] correspond with these two. Wind, after studying medicine and living in the States is at present in Winnipeg where up to its demise he edited the Yiddish

Vort, a weekly. Beller, now in his eighties, lives in Israel. He spent much of his life in Argentina and he would write correspondences about South American countries for the *Globe and Mail* after yours truly would translate them. There was one year particularly rich in the usual Latin American *coups d'etat* and Beller always had an article ready from his wide repertoire on any given Latin American country be it Peru, Brazil or Equador.

Before Shapiro was Rhinewine, who came from Mezritch in Russian Poland, a man who managed to do some original research on Canadian Jewish history including the story of Ezekiel Hart. It's a typical story of how rigid party lines were in those days that in 1930 when Sam Factor ran for Parliament in what was later to be Spadina riding and the *Journal* supported him, Rhinewine was ostracized by the socialist party he belonged to, as he was guilty of supporting a bourgeois capitalist candidate. Paradoxically, Rhinewine, who had come from the ranks of the Socialist Territorialists, was the author of a book on *Eretz Yisroel* in Jewish literature. Territorialists were people who were perceived to look elsewhere than to Palestine for the Jewish solution.

Before Rhinewine's untimely death at forty-four in 1931, there was a breach in the ranks, a quarrel between him and Shapiro, the details of which I am not familiar with, and it led eventually to a new Yiddish publication, a weekly named *Keneder Neies* which was published and edited by Maurice Goldstick and his sister Mrs. Dorothy Dworkin. This was not sold across the counter but was distributed as an insert with the weekend edition of the New York Yiddish papers of which Mrs. Dworkin was the distributing agent. This newsheet managed to satisfy both major ideological elements in the Jewish community and performed the uncommon feat of being both pro-Bundist and pro-Zionist at the same time. Pro-Bundist, because Mrs. Dworkin continued the tradition of her late husband Henry Dworkin who was active in the Socialist movement, and Zionist because Goldstick was a devoted Zionist. Both ideologies had in common a fervid anti-Communism. Those who didn't see eye to eye with the paper called it the *mamzerel*. Why? Because like a *mamzer* it was *untergevorfn, i.e.,* it was tossed in gratis with the New York papers. Its life span as I calculate it was twenty years from 1935 to about 1955.

Before Gershon Pomerantz undertook the editorship of the *Hebrew Journal* which he did in its last two years as a regularly appearing daily newspaper he had already experimented in seven careers. Since coming to Toronto about 1930 he had conducted a Yiddish lending library, been an insurance agent, been employed by Canadian Jewish Congress as secretary to its "Peoples Division", owned a printing business, been a publisher of Yiddish books by distinguished authors like Leivik and Opatoshu, and during all these livelihoods had *"untergezindikt mit'n pen,"* *i.e.,* had written Yiddish poetry which appeared in various anthologies. He also contributed essays to the *Freie Arbeiter Shtimme* in New York under the pseudonym of A. Sokolover. After all these abortive attempts at a livelihood he went into building contracting and for a brief period was actually a *g'veer.* He, by the way, had a mop of hair, a *chuprina,* that was more luxuriant than Shapiro's. Though always interested in Yiddish he had always disdained the local daily in that language and once when I saw him buying one, in some embarrassment he explained that he bought it only for that particular paper. At one time he confided in me that he was planning to publish an English language Jewish paper, a weekly. He had the name chosen—*The Jewish Nation*—and had gone as far as a dummy front page which he showed me. This was in his printing period when he possessed the machinery to do it. But nothing came of it. Eventually he became editor of the paper he had professed to disdain and as a *zetzer,* a linotype operator (another one of his *parnosses*), he would typeset the editorials right into the hot type. He thoroughly enjoyed this position: denouncing and criticising right and left, reprinting his literary criticism and poems and reviews, and putting out the entire paper himself. He even modernized the spelling, bringing the *Journal* up to date in its old age. But eventually ill-health caught up to him and he had to give up.

Before I leave the *Journal,* let me say something about its English page, a feature it acquired in the late 1930s. Its first editor was Moses Frank. A man of many talents and many languages, he was at home in Russian, Yiddish, Hebrew and English and wrote professionally in at least three of these four. Like Shmuel Mayer Shapiro he was from Belorussia and a Litvak but totally different in temperament. He was primarily a Hebrew writer and it was in that language that he probably preferred to write. He graduated from the Ontario College of Education and had a high school teacher's diploma but Jewish teachers were not being hired in those days. He was principal of the Brunswick Avenue Talmud Torah, the city's best regarded Hebrew school. He had also been an ill-paid executive-secretary at the Canadian Jewish Congress in those days when the salary was from $10 to $15 a week out of which you also paid the stenographer. He was also for a while up to 1937 publisher-editor of the *Jewish Standard*. And the last of these *parnosses* before he left Canada, and by no means the most glorious of them, was when he was editor—the first I believe—of the English page of the *Journal*. He also wrote a column along the side of the page commenting on the day's news.

When he went to the States I would see his name in the *Forverts* attached to reviews of Hebrew books and articles of a general nature. And I saw his name as well in *Hadoar*, the Hebrew weekly, and much later in Gabriel Cohen's *National Jewish Post* at which time he held a public relations job with the city of Haifa. Moses Frank and his wife died in a car accident while visiting Montreal in 1977. His son Reuven Frank, now sixty-one, is president of the NBC-TV News Corporation, a leading member of the Eastern News Establishment that Spiro Agnew so vigorously attacked some years ago.

The next holder of this English-page editorship was the distinguished David Rome, later to become the noted archivist, historian and librarian that he is today. It's not generally known that he used to be a Torontonian; this was after he left Vancouver but before he settled in Montreal where he was to achieve his true level of accomplishment. Mr. Rome served from January 1940 to November 1942. He was followed by Ben Lappin who held the position for one year. Leo Hayman (younger brother to Julius),

City politicians understood that the Jewish press was the best way to reach the Jewish masses before an election. Left, ad for Joseph Singer for member of Parliament, Canadian Jewish Review, October 1925. Right, Hebrew Journal ad promoting Nathan Phillips for alderman in Ward Four in election for 1941.

Rabbi H. Goodman (who wrote under the *nom de plume* of Ben Tuvim) and Nathan Cohen were also editors.

The *Journal*, I must admit, never had the prestige that its Montreal counterpart the *Adler* enjoyed. Israel Rabinowitz, the *Adler* editor, was a much wider known figure in the world of Jewish culture than Shapiro and I stress the word "Jewish" rather than "Yiddish," for Rabinowitz was an authority on Jewish music. The *Journal* didn't gather around itself a literary coterie comparable to a Melech Ravitch, a B. G. Sack, an I. J. Segal or the many other notable names including, by the way, the early Conrad Bercovici. But that probably is reflective of the gap that then existed between the two cities and the two Jewish communities. The *Journal* never pretended to be anything more than what it was—a provincial daily serving the needs and interests of a very local public.

There was also a third Yiddish paper in Toronto that I recall. It was officially considered a New York paper, yet the advertising and much of the writing, editing and printing was done in Toronto. This was the *Proletarisher Gedank*, the organ of a very small minority group, the left Poalei Zion. We have a bound set of a year's copies for 1933–34 at the cjc office in Toronto where the spelling is in the Soviet style with Hebrew words spelled out phonetically though halfway through the set the spelling reverts to the traditional orthography. And the ideology reflected this split personality:

62

the Soviet Union was praised for its socialist achievement but the *Yevsekess*, the Jewish communists, both there and here in Canada, were denounced in unequivocal terms. And there was a class-conscious article denouncing the about-to-be-recognized Canadian Jewish Congress as a tool of the Jewish exploiting bourgeoisie. Only a decade later these same men, the Max Federmans and Harry Simons and Moishe Menachovskys were very much part of the Canadian Jewish Congress and were its most loyal supporters.

The Jewish or rather Yiddish-speaking communist movement in Toronto has a long history of having a press organ. More than any other grouping within the diversified Jewish community they would feel the need of a separate organ. They were so distinctly different in their ideology from all the other factions that they couldn't expect what they'd consider as fair treatment in a general "*klal Yisroel*" publication, so they always had their own paper. Besides which they needed their own organ for political reasons. Their first paper was called, appropriately, *Der Kamf* ("The Struggle") and its first editor was Philip Halpern. He died in 1932. My grandfather's tombstone is a few steps away from the UJPO cemetery section and it's fascinating to read the inscription on the tombstones of their stalwarts—including Philip Halpern's. The inscriptions are in Yiddish, not the traditional Hebrew: sometimes they take the form of long poems and are full of dedication to the cause of improved humanity, the ideal of the proletariat, a classless society, a "*sheneren morgen,*" the world revolution, etcetera, echoes of the slogans of bygone days.

In 1939 when the Stalin-Hitler pact was in operation and the party was illegal the name of the paper was changed to *Der Veg*. After the war, when the Communist Party was respectable, at least for a few years, the name *Vochenblatt* was adopted—a rather colourless name without the militancy or challenge of *Der Kamf*. The editors included Sam Lipshitz (who left the Party after the 1956 revelations). The long-time editor who stuck with the UJPO was Joshua Gershman and when his health failed about two or three years ago, the paper stopped publishing. It was not, of course,

The Yiddish-speaking masses turned to the Yiddish dailies to learn what was happening in the city and the wider world. Front page of Hebrew Journal of January 3, 1928, announcing Sam McBride's election as mayor of Toronto.

self-sustaining. Gershman himself would take a Canada-wide trip once or twice a year to raise funds to keep it going. The contributors and co-editors included the cartoonist Avrom Yanofsky (who also wrote), Harry Guralnick, Joe Salsberg (until his departure from the Party) and Sholem Shtern of Montreal, the noted poet. Nathan Cohen, later to become the acclaimed theatre critic, was editor of its English page in the late 1940s. The most interesting series I recall reading was that written by Joe Salsberg in 1956 in six or eight instalments detailing his various visits to the Soviet Union and how they led to his eventual renunciation of his former links.

It is difficult now and in English to evoke the personal and ideological fire of Canada's Yiddish-language journalism. Perhaps one experience of my own out of the recent past can recapture the flavour. In 1956—I was then on the staff of the Canadian Jewish Congress—I had just returned from a trip to Winnipeg. Shortly afterwards there appeared an article in *Vochenblatt*, the communist weekly, by Gershman making his periodic commentary on the news. First there was the ritual denunciation of Max Federman, the traitor, the tool of the bosses, the labour renegade, besides whom

64

העלפט קאנאדע זיין געזונט

HELP CANADA KEEP FIT

Girl — possibly a Girl Guide — says "Oh Mama, this is the dish for me!" Ad for Nabisco Shredded Wheat, Hebrew Journal, 1928.

there was no one lower. This was nothing new. Mr. Federman, a labour organizer active in the fur-trade unions, was always notably and vocally anti-communist, and had been considered public enemy number one by them since the crowbar-wielding days on Spadina Avenue. But this time the attack was different. Someone had been found who was even lower than Mr. Federman and these were the exact words used: *"S'iz do eyner vos er iz nideriker fun Federman!"* ("There is someone who is even lower than Federman!") I read on impatiently to see who this unspeakable wretch could be. And there it was, in large bold type, *"Un dos iz Ben Kayfetz!"* It was me he was writing about! There followed a denunciation of me coupled with a real offbeat and far-out interpretation of why I had been sent by my Canadian Jewish Congress masters to Winnipeg (supposedly to change the community's mind on the issue of West Germany's rearmament, but actually that had nothing to do with my assignment). From that point on I had the edge on Max Federman whenever I saw him: I was proud of my distinction—to be lower than Federman was no mean achievement, as I assured him!

Page of political ads in Hebrew Journal preceding municipal election, 1928.
Nathan Phillips appears at upper right, Sol Eisen and David Goldstick at upper
left, Ian MacDonnell at lower right.

What was happening in the meantime in the English-
language Jewish press? Not very much, I am constrained to say,
at least not until 1930. The *Canadian Jewish Review* had been
founded in Toronto in 1921 by George and Florence Freedlander
Cohen, two emigres from across the border in Buffalo, New York.
This was a publication that paid great attention to genteel society
notes—comings and goings to the Catskills, the Adirondacks and
the Laurentians, detailed descriptions of what the bride wore (a

recurring phrase was "pulled in at the bodice"), who held the baby boy at the *bris*, and who poured tea at any given reception (cocktail parties were out as this was still under Prohibition). I recall one particular social note that gave a perfect picture of what a social scientist would call not "upward" but "lateral mobility." It read like this: "Mrs. A. Nussbaum and her daughter Elaine have moved their residence from 12 St. Andrew Street to 26 Leonard Avenue." The family name and street numbers have been changed but the street names are those actually mentioned in the social note. Those of you who are familiar with the geography of the old Ward Four South area in Toronto will get the message. The move is from the address in the old Jewish quarter to another, three or four blocks distant— and equally unfashionable.

Soon after Ontario introduced the government-supervised sale of liquor but, unlike Quebec, still did not permit its commercial advertising, the *Review* moved its main office (as did other periodicals) from Toronto to Montreal to take advantage of this advertising revenue. It now became a two-city weekly, establishing a precedent which has been followed today by the *Canadian Jewish News*.

Florence Friedlander Cohen was known by her initials as FFC. The masthead bore a little doggerel poem:

Sometimes when people censure me
I tell them without rancour,
For what it costs me to be free
I could have had an anchor.

Although the poem may give the impression that she was a fighting, crusading journalist, nothing could be further from the truth. A year could go by—sometimes longer—with no editorial whatsoever. When she did get sufficiently riled up she could pen a vigorous paragraph, but it happened rarely. The *Review* did not pursue much of an editorial policy in Jewish politics. What it did subscribe to was a mild non-Zionism, even extending sometimes to anti-Zionism, reflecting perhaps the middle-class, culturally assimilitated, older generation and "classical Reform" American background of its founders. You have to keep in mind that non-Zionism was quite acceptable in those days. The American Jewish Committee and its leadership, the Louis Marshalls and the Sulzbergers, and the American Jewish establishment in general were all non-Zionists. B'nai Brith was non-Zionist; most of the Reform rabbis were non-Zionist including Rabbi Eisendrath who came to Holy Blossom in 1929 and who contributed a column each week to the *Review.*

Another point—the front page of the *Canadian Jewish Review* rarely if ever had carried any Canadian Jewish news. It was all culled from the pages of the *New York Times* listing the benefactions or the deaths of various American Jewish philanthropists. The only Canadian news I recall it featuring was when the noted physician Dr. I. Rabinowitz delivered his notorious anti-Zionist address to the Canadian Club in Montreal in 1946.

The attacks on the Jews at the Western Wall and in Hebron in 1929 put the entire Jewish world in turmoil. In Toronto, however, Rabbi Eisendrath reprimanded the Zionists who in some way were held responsible for the attacks and this was reflected in his column in the *Review.* The Zionists, led by Mrs. Rose Dunkelman, were terribly frustrated. There was nowhere that the Zionist point of view could be put forward in the English language to reach the English-speaking Jews and the general non-Jewish Canadian public. What did she do? She started her own paper, and in 1930 begins the history of the *Jewish Standard.*

Meyer Weisgal, the man who was brought in to be the voice of Zionism in Toronto was truly a remarkable figure, someone who was larger than life and was destined to play a larger role in world Jewry and Zionism. He had been serving as editor of *The New Palestine*, organ of the Zionist Organization of America where he was continually getting into trouble for exceeding his budget and making extravagant payments to highly paid writers like Winston Churchill and David Lloyd George. He most assuredly made an impact on Toronto and on Toronto Jewish journalism in the two years that he lived in the city. He continued his practice of inviting world famous writers and in the next few years the *Jewish Standard* ran original commissioned articles by such noted celebrities as Dorothy Thompson, Pierre Van Paassen, Winston Churchill. He used his ZOA contacts to get writers like Louis Lipsky, Felix Frankfurter, Nahum Sokolow and Menachem Ussishkin. Weisgal was not yet the right-hand man to Chaim Weizmann that he was to become but he was already a defender of his ideas. I recall a two-page spread in the *Standard* with a large portrait of Vladimir Jabotinsky on one side and one of Chaim Weizmann on the other—two men who held opposing views on the way Zionist politics and diplomacy were to be directed. The article upholding Jabotinsky was written by Archie Bennett and the article defending Weizmann was by Weisgal. I recall Weisgal once addressing a Young Judaea assembly. He made some remark mentioning the impact Herzl had made upon him. I immediately assumed he had been contemporary to Herzl and had seen him—after all he was a member of the "older" generation, possibly about fifty. I was thirteen or fourteen and anyone over thirty was a "senior citizen." It was years later that I realized that Weisgal was only thirty when he spoke to us and was himself a child when Herzl died.

Weisgal in two short years had put the *Jewish Standard* on the world Jewish map, attracting the ablest, most popular writers. It was truly an international journal of the highest level which happened to be published in Toronto. But it wasn't meant to last. The Depression of the 1930s and Weisgal's free hand with money were two mutually incompatible factors. Eventually, as he relates in his memoirs, Mrs. Dunkelman confided in him that the cupboard was bare and he left Toronto to do other things. He became the organizer and impresario for a Jewish pageant at the Chicago World Fair of 1933 where he made his reputation as a showman. Later he was to make a reputation as a master fund-raiser for the Weizmann Institute of Science.

After that the *Standard* steadily went downhill. There was a Meyer Steinglass who was editor but of whom I had no personal experience. The ownership went through many vicissitudes and changeovers in the five years between 1932 and 1937. It was sold to non-Jewish publishing firms—J. Laird Thompson, the Age Publishing Company on Willcocks Street, and for a while it was one of the Maclean-Hunter stable of periodicals. It then fell into the hands of Moses Z. Frank whom we mentioned earlier. Frank was a good editor but not as good a businessman. In 1937 Julius Hayman, then thirty years old, a newcomer from Winnipeg who had been its business manager and had started a rival periodical, the *Jewish Sentinel*, bought the *Standard* from Frank for under $1,000 and finally brought stability to the publication as its editor-publisher for the next forty-five years, which double position he still holds.

In 1941 I was employed by the *Jewish Standard*. This was well after Julius Hayman had obtained control. My job was a melange of advertising salesman, article writer, proofreader, and sub-editor. I did everything but the printing. On one occasion I "borrowed" an article from another periodical in the best tradition of Anglo-Jewish journalism but in my lack of experience I neglected to ask permission of the author or provide him with an honourarium. Whereupon Mr. Hayman received a threatening communication from the author, a certain Alfred Werner, a recent refugee from Germany who probably needed the money. But did he need as much as $500, which was what he demanded? I was quite alarmed as this situation was new to me and I was concerned about how the publisher would extricate himself. But Mr. Hayman was very cool. He waited a few weeks until Mr. Werner, too, cooled off somewhat. Then he sent him a cheque for $5. We never heard from Mr. Werner again.

There was a long period through the 1940s and 1950s when Toronto had no English language Jewish weekly. The *Jewish Standard* was at various times a monthly and a fortnightly but never a weekly, and *The Review* had moved to Montreal. It was in 1960, when M. J. Nurenberger switched languages, that we enter the current period with the founding of the *Canadian Jewish News*.

A very important personality of the Jewish press in Toronto—or for that matter in all of Canada—has so far been overlooked. I

70

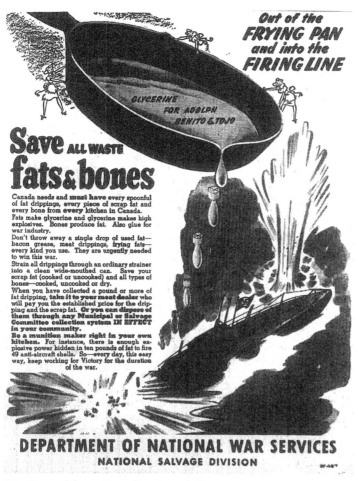

Wartime ad from Canadian Jewish Review, 1943

refer to Archie Bennett, who towered so tall over so many others. Archie was so many other things and wore so many other *hitlekh* (I daren't say yarmulkas because of his well-known anti-yarmulka campaign of the 1960s). He was first and foremost a community leader and a major businessman; though many didn't realize it, he and his brothers pioneered in the building of shopping centres or plazas in Canada back in the 1950s. Only after all this was he a journalist, who played at it as it were and dabbled with his column. Well, that may be the way some of us perceived it but not the way he saw it. The ballot for the election of Toronto delegates to the first assembly of the Canadian Jewish Congress in 1919 identified all the candidates by their occupation. And what do you think he was tagged as? As a journalist of course and probably very proudly.

First in a series of "Bits of Yiddish" cartoons that appeared in the Canadian Jewish Standard, 1935.

I think what he most dearly wanted to be in this world, next to teaching philosophy at Queens, was a working full-time journalist. Archie was probably the first bilingual Jewish journalist Canada had. He used to contribute to *Keneder Adler* when his friend A. A. Roback was editor and he wrote ponderous essays on Old English literature, *i.e.,* the Anglo-Saxon epics, probably the only time in history this subject was ever dealt with in that language. Also he was the first truly national journalist we had in the East. Being raised in Kingston he was open to both Toronto and Montreal. He wrote for the old *Jewish Times* of Montreal, the *Jewish Chronicle* of Montreal, the *Jewish Review* both when it was in Toronto and Montreal, and for the *Jewish Standard* of Toronto. As a young man in the summer intervals from Queens he was editor of the *Canadian Jewish Times* in Montreal so he was not merely an amateur dabbler when he dubbed himself a "journalist" on that Congress ballot.

In his prime, Archie Bennett's writing style was much more interesting than his speaking style. One could enjoy his writing more than his speaking. For one thing, his wit shone through his writing much more lucidly. His speaking suffered from an unfortunate muffled mumble which was very irritating and which more than once aroused an audience to protest. He loved to coin words, to build little verbal castles in the air, to wind phrases up and down and in and out of an imaginary labyrinth, and his satiric jousts were delightful. Some day an enterprising editor or publisher will collect the best of his columns and put them together in book form. They will form a fascinating picture of Canadian Jewry as Archie saw it from the second to the seventh decade of this century. And he was never without a column. All the time from 1912 to only several years before his passing in 1981 he was never without a vehicle to express himself—and we are the richer for it.

What did he write about? He wrote about the *landsmanshaften* and the sick benefit societies which used to dot the Jewish horizon. He wrote about his friends Moses and Louis Gelber, always making the point in a patronizing but kindly fashion that after all one must remember they were Galicianer. He carried on his anti-yarmulka campaign—not, *cholila*, that he was against the yarmulka per se or was anti-religious. What he vigorously opposed was the tyranny and regimentation in the new postwar congregations, the imposing of the Yarmulka Only rule, the ban against the fedora, the derby or the peak cap for which he saw no sanction in Torah or *halakha*. He wrote about Sam Kronick and Sam's partner in charity, Willy Agranove. He wrote about communism, about Zionism, about Weizmann, about Jabotinsky, about his contemporaries Ben Sadowski and Irving Oelbaum, Mike Garber and Sam Bronfman, about the Canadian Jewish Congress and the philosophy of Congress. He and S. M. Shapiro were the most ardent exponents of this philosophy of a Jewish populism that arose during and after World War One. He wrote about Herzl, Stephen Wise and Chayim Greenberg. But above all he wrote about Reuben Brainin who in his Montreal years gathered around him a group of *talmidim* and

Advertisements for films, especially if they had Jewish content, often appeared in the Jewish press. Left, ad for The House of Rothschild, motion picture starring George Arliss, Boris Karloff, Loretta Young and Robert Young, Canadian Jewish Standard, 1934. Right, ad for Power, a dramatization of Lion Feuchtwanger's novel Jew Suss, Canadian Jewish Standard, 1934.

chassidim, an intellectual coterie. It was an experience that was Archie's own personal renaissance and *risorgimento* wrapped into one. Archie never forgot or let his readers forget his debt to this intellectual leader and inspirer. And this too was directly linked to the Jewish press, as it was as editor of the *Keneder Adler* that Brainin owed his presence in Montreal and Canada.

There were various other personalities marginally linked with the Toronto Jewish press. Cantor Nathan Stolnitz would come to me to translate his writings into a passable English for eventual publication in a book on Jewish music and cantorial *nigguna* in which the author's photo would invariably appear in the company of a Koussevitsky or a Richard Tucker or a Leibele Waldman or a Pintchik or one or another of the *chazzanic* celebrities or even a Bobby Breen. There was Israel Plattner who couldn't let a word escape his lips without a pun, a quip, a play on words, generally betwixt English and Yiddish. Plattner and Stolnitz both contributed to the *Journal*, Plattner also doing the occasional poetic effort. Plattner suffered from the illusion that the only obstacle preventing him from achieving the success of a George Kaufman, a Lerner

74

and Loewe or any other famous Broadway lyricist was the lack of a proper translator. He had had it from Yankev Kalich himself, who was Molly Picon's husband, that if his *chochmes* were put into English he'd be the toast of Broadway. Plattner died blind with diabetes and confined to a wheelchair at the Baycrest Hospital where I would visit him, but to the end he never gave up his playing with words and toying with language.

One contributor to the Toronto Yiddish press, S. Nepom, came to my acquaintance in a most unusual way without my having the slightest idea he was a Yiddish poet and in a milieu far removed from the usual ambiance of the litterateurs. He was a streetcar conductor whose base was the TTC car barns at Roncesvalles and Queen Street overlooking Sunnyside. I knew he was a man who was well read as he would talk to me from time to time about Bernard Shaw and would nod knowingly. The other TTC conductors and motormen held him in great awe as a man who could handle several languages including French which he had acquired in Montreal. Years later I came across his name in an anthology of Canadian Yiddish poems that he wrote for the *Adler*, the *Journal* and the leftist *Kamf*. His tombstone is located in the UJPO section of the Dawes Road *beis oylem*.

Despite the rhetoric of the Yiddishists, the Yiddish press in Canada is receding into the past and the English-language Jewish press has become more of an impersonal nationwide operation. I am rather pleased, looking back at it, that I was around in the era when journalism was still a business for individuals. Do not misunderstand what I am saying. I am not looking back nostalgically to a better day. The public, I am sure, is better served today. But while it lasted, it was enjoyable, and I am delighted that I can recall such episodes. ∽

Panoramic photo of Trades & Labour Congress, London, Ontario, September 1933, attended by J. B. Salsberg (close-up on opposite page).

J. B. Salsberg—Charismatic 'Man of the People'

THE TIME WAS AUGUST 1913—twelve months before the Great Conflagration would engulf Europe and leave the Western world badly battered and radically altered. It was as though the small group of four—Sarah-Gittel Salsberg, her son Yossele and daughters Pearl and Lil in tow—had some premonition of the disaster to come when they set their goal for Canada, saying goodbye to Poland. In fact she was a reluctant traveller and it had not been an easy decision. There had already been one false start which had gotten them as far as the seaport and then back to Lagow.

Abraham Salsberg, too, had to weigh the matter. So much so that he, who was already in Canada, had crossed the ocean twice. The first time he had returned, not being impressed with the godliness of this new land. But back in Poland the outlook grew worse and he returned to Canada, this time to stay. And after a few years he sent *shifskarten*—steamship tickets—for his wife and children to follow. He had purchased a house on Cecil Street just east of Spadina and all was ready for their arrival.

For Sarah-Gittel it was an even harder choice. She was unwilling to leave. In Lagow she was a *balebosta*, mistress of a household with some standing in the community and among her peers. Most of her kinfolk were in Poland and there was a strong bond between them. She sensed that once she left she would never see them again. And she never did see them again. A Chassidic rebbe in another town was consulted and on the strength of his advice the decision was made. But it was not with a sense of joyful

From Canadian Kupat-Holim tribute booklet, Toronto 1991.

77

The Ostrovtzer Synagogue, Cecil Street just east of Spadina, 1966. The Salsberg family lived across the street. (Speisman)

anticipation that the foursome embarked from Danzig on the ship that was to carry them to Canada.

Arriving in Toronto by train from Halifax, the mother and three children disembarked at the Old Union Station opposite Simcoe Street. They engaged not a taxicab to take them to their destination but a horse cab. To Sarah Gittel, a horse-drawn vehicle seemed more reliable and able to withstand traffic than a newfangled mechanical motor contraption.

Although Spadina Avenue was not yet the intensively Jewish thoroughfare it was to become in the 1920s and the centre of Jewish gravity was still to the east in St. John's Ward, Jewish settlers were already moving into the adjacent streets: Cecil, Nassau, Oxford, Baldwin, D'Arcy. Shortly after the end of the decade the church directly opposite the Salsberg home at 73 Cecil Street was transformed into the Great Synagogue of Ostrovtze and further down Spadina another church became the Anshei England congregation, that bulwark of Empire among his Majesty's loyal Jewish subjects. Later when he was earning some money Joe put down a deposit of $500 to purchase a larger, more commodious house further east at 59 Cecil Street.

Once in Canada young Yossele was sent to public school, the institution being Lansdowne School on Spadina Crescent (now

Left, Joe's parents, Abraham & Sarah-Gittel Salsberg, from Eitz Chaim Talmud Torah anniversary book, 1943. Centre, Salsberg brothers Bob, J. B. and Nat in the army. Right, J. B. as photographed by a Queen Street studio in the 1920s.

ennobled as Lord Lansdowne). Joe spent only two years there and entered the work force at the early age of thirteen, taking his bar-mitzvah rite of passage quite literally. His parents had more children: Nathan, Bob, Thelma and Betty.

Before long Spadina Avenue took over the Jewish hegemony from the Ward which gradually turned into an incipient Chinatown (as would happen to Spadina itself some fifty years later). Within a few years there were a number of Jewish shops in the area and a number of better stores, one of these being the Walker store just below College Street. Young Joe would carry out errands such as buying hairnets for his mother and going by bicycle to Eaton's to buy twenty-five cents' worth of perfume for his mother which the sales clerk would insert into a bottle by means of an eye-dropper. One of Yossele's early errand-boy jobs was with the *Hebrew Daily Journal*, thus exposing him at an early age to the politics of Jewish journalism.

Father had been a baker in *der heym*—a well-paid unionized trade in Canada. Why, then, had he not pursued that skill in Toronto? Because of his essential sense of integrity. He could see "cutting corners" and dishonesty in the trade. Bakers would start functioning several hours before sundown on Saturday afternoon to ensure fresh-baked rolls and bread for their public for Saturday evening and as a colleague the pressure was on him to do likewise. He could not compromise his piety or his integrity; consequently he abandoned the baker's trade and became self-employed as a peddler of second-hand goods, a common livelihood among immigrant

Jews who were not ready to relinquish their way of life. As a self-employed person he could observe the Sabbath and festivals without being beholden to an employer.

The Talmud Torah Eitz Chaim 25th anniversary book of 1943 lists Abraham Salsberg as among those who were the founders of this institution. In 1922 he was on its executive committee. Sarah-Gittel's main communal interest was the Halboshes Arumim Society, the women's auxiliary of the Eitz Chaim Talmud Torah whose specific commitment, following the name which translated as "to clothe the naked," was to provide appropriate and adequate clothing for children whose parents were destitute.

Rabbi Nachman Shemen, the noted author and former teacher and principal at the school, told me: "If anyone came to Sarah-Gittel and asked a favour, it was granted immediately. And J. B. may not have inherited the religious ideology of his parents but he did inherit their rules of human behaviour."

At the Eitz Chaim each teacher was asked to make a list of those pupils who lacked proper clothing. Their sizes in shoes and basic items of apparel were obtained and they were fitted out for new clothing at tailors on Queen Street West or Spadina Avenue who contributed their services and wares either gratis or at a liberal discount. Occasionally there would be an ethical and moral problem: should they accept offers of clothing from retailers or wholesalers who kept their shops open on the Sabbath? The entire procedure was carried out with great discretion to avoid embarrassing or singling out individual boys and girls.

Sarah-Gittel remained president of the Halboshes Arumim to her dying day. In later years, when the problem of clothing for the poor was abated, the funds were used for general charitable purposes.

The older Salsberg could be called a "*tehillim-yid.*" In a crisis he would seek superior guidance in the recital of the Psalms. The late Rabbi J. L. Graubart once remarked jokingly: "With his *tehillim* saying Reb Avrohom may eventually get his son elected."

In the years before the Eitz Chaim Talmud Torah was erected

on D'Arcy Street the *shtiebl* that Abraham Salsberg attended was in a run-down structure on Chestnut Street with outside plumbing, next door to the Galician congregation Shomrei Shabbos. It was called Chevra Tomchei Shabbos. A group of members' sons, Joe among them, would conduct their own services in another room of the house, calling themselves the Tifereth Bachurim. And in whatever spare time there was, Joe would apply himself informally to Torah study under the tutelage of older learned men, B'nai Torah they were called, who saw this as fulfilling a vital mitzvah on their part. Joe's Torah study never left him and to this day his speech is peppered with Talmudic allusions.

Great hopes were laid upon the head of Joseph, the first born in the family. It was the hope of his parents that he would proceed in the ways of Torah and eventually study for the rabbinate. But that was not meant to be. For one thing, Joe felt the obligation to help support the growing family. He was twelve years older than the first Canadian-born child in the family, and he keenly felt this moral obligation. He very early took a job in the rag trade, starting at $3 and working up to $5 a week. From this point there was no looking back. For another thing, 1917 was a year of two cataclysmic events, the Balfour Declaration and the Russian Revolution. Joe became one of a group of young Poalei Zion who were inspired by the twin doctrines of Socialism and Zionism, a group that met in a building on Spadina and St. Andrew Street on the site of the later Labour Lyceum. It was in this movement that he met his contemporaries, Samuel B. (later Dr.) Hurwich, union leader Chaim Langer and Izzy Weinrot.

To his pious father this was another form of *apikorsus*, of heresy, a deviation from the paths of the true faith. Joe tells the story of how his father came to spy him out at a Poalei Zion meeting where the renowned Yiddish poet David Pinsky was the guest. Joe had been forewarned and sentinels had been posted at the doors to watch for the elder Salsberg's arrival. When they signalled that he was near, Joe dived under a table where he would not be visible to anyone looking in from the door. A position of little dignity to be sure, especially for

Composite photo of members of Poalei Zion Youth Club, Toronto 1918. Salsberg is in bottom row, second from left.

one who had been given the honour of introducing David Pinsky, but the ruse was preferable to the ignominy and embarrassment of being led out by the ear in the presence of his peers.

At one point Abraham sent his wayward son to the newly arrived spiritual leader of the Eitz Chaim, Rabbi J. L. Graubart, who, it was hoped, would dissuade him from his radical ways. But the learned and astute rabbi made no such attempt; the two had a pleasant chat together.

On one occasion Joe was given the final ultimatum. "I can no longer control you," said the father, "and for the sake of the younger children, you must conform or leave!" Joe sadly gathered up his belongings including a dozen Yiddish books: he had become a devotee of Yiddish letters, something the Orthodox regarded as *bitul Torah*, a distraction from true learning. He was about to move in with a friend until he found permanent lodgings when a great-aunt intruded—an aunt of his mother to whom she always deferred, and the day was saved. Joe was never a demonstrative *apikoros*. He at all times respected religion and religious practice and had great respect for his father, "the most honest man I have ever met in all my life." From that point on there was a truce effected: neither tried to convince or convert the other.

Joe's organizational talents in the Poalei Zion were soon recognized and he was invited to come to New York and take the post of secretary general of the Young Poalei Zion of America, a position that put him in direct contact with the leadership and mainstream of North American Zionist politics. Among his duties was the editing of two party publications, one of these in Yiddish called *Yugnt-zhurnal*. Though never a professional or full-time journalist he was to develop a talent and taste for writing for the press that was to accompany him throughout all the vicissitudes of his career. The New York episode did not last longer than a year.

The Poalei Zion movement, like all Socialist movements at that juncture in history, was embroiled in the left–right controversy, a controversy thrown up by the October Revolution and what flowed from it: to be aligned with the Third International, siding with the Soviet Union, or to stand with the Social Democratic Second International? Joe was inclined to the former and grew close to the Left Poalei Zion, a party that then tried to adjust to the two axes of Moscow and Jerusalem.

Returning to Toronto, he was at a crossroads and he determined to complete his unfinished formal education and enter the university. But he did it the hard way—working at the London Hat Company on Lombard Street during the day and studying for matriculation by night. He was given private tuition by a Harbord Collegiate teacher. On the wall over his workplace was a sheet of paper with Latin verb declensions and conjugations which he repeated by rote as pupils have done for centuries. But fate stepped in by way of an offer he could not see himself refusing—to become the organizer for the locals of the Hat, Cap and Millinery Workers Union of North America for the city of Chicago. That was the end of any plans to enter university. From that point on he was immersed in labour and socialist politics.

Chicago of the early 1920s was a rough, rude and upsetting experience for the young idealist. It was the era of Prohibition when lawlessness, brutality, corruption, terror and murder were commonplace. The racketeers not only dominated liquor, drugs and gambling but invaded the labour unions, exacting tribute from neighbourhood Mom and Pop retailers. Joe was involved in directing a strike and one night around midnight while riding home on a streetcar, a bullet crashed through the window where he sat. It was clearly an attempt on his life, his friends, who knew Chicago better, explained. He was advised to leave Chicago for a while.

In Chicago Joe and Dora were married. Dora Wilensky, a Toronto-based social worker, had received her Jewish education at the Peretz Shul; her parents were Workmen's Circle members. She was to build an enviable reputation as executive director of the Jewish Family and Child Service of Toronto and built that agency to the place it holds today in public estimation.

While in Chicago Joe moved further to the left. He found that the mainstream of the labour movement in the States was to the right and there was much in their policies he could not accept.

In the end it was the British General Strike of 1926 that impelled him to cross his Rubicon and formally and publicly enter the Communist Party. His die was cast. He was convinced that only the Communists held the key to the redemption of the worker. There was, as well, a Jewish consideration. The reports of Yiddish schools established in the Soviet Union, the encouragement and sponsorship of Yiddish literature and the publication of Yiddish books by government agencies in White Russia and the Ukraine were to him a clear signal that here at last was a regime that cared for and even identified with Jewish culture. Not the traditional religious culture, since there was no presence of Hebrew, but secularism was

Cover and inside page of Salsberg's 1939 membership booklet for the Communist Party of Canada, which he joined in 1926 and famously broke away from more than thirty years later because of Russia's horrendous treatment of Jews.

the wave of the future. This was more than any other regime had ever attempted. Truly a noble experiment, he believed, and one that deserved full support.

The story of Joseph Salsberg for the next thirty years is fully identified with his attachment to the Communist Party. His particular responsibility was the trade union field and for more than twenty years he headed the party's trade union department, a task which took him to all parts of Canada, bringing him in touch with industrialists, labour lawyers, trade unionists and politicians of every stripe. He was considered the number two man in the Party.

But Joe never gave up his personal interest in the Jewish branches and in Jewish life. He wrote for the *Tribune* and its earlier incarnations, the *Clarion* and *Worker*. He conducted a weekly column in the Yiddish *Kamf* and later wrote from time to time in the *Vochenblatt*. For the latter he would often write the same article in two languages, translating himself. He was at all times available as a speaker at Party and non-Party functions—a miners' strike, an anniversary of Mendele Mocher Sforim, a picnic at Camp Naivelt in Eldorado Park.

Salsberg, it should be stated, was not at all times a subservient

Party member accepting unquestioningly the diktat from above. During the Lovestonite quarrels of 1929 he was considered a dissenter and was suspended from the Party. But he stayed close to pro-Soviet activity, taking a post as secretary of the Canadian Friends of the Soviet Union. In a year's time he returned to the Party.

Back in Toronto, Salsberg first ran for public office in the municipal elections of 1935 and was defeated. He was a candidate again in 1936 and again was defeated though polling a slightly higher vote. He ran a third time in 1937, raising his vote but not by enough to win. Later the same year he ran in the provincial balloting for St. Andrew riding and came within 151 votes of victory. Finally, on New Year's Day 1938 he was elected alderman.

But he was not returned on New Year's day of 1939. A strong anti-Communist campaign by David Balfour and a misguided Party decision to place a second pro-Communist candidate in the Board of Education race to oust Herbert Oriliffe served to antagonize a large number of voters and Joe failed to be re-elected.

What were the issues in the 1938 Toronto City Council? It was still a Depression year, Mackenzie King was in power in Ottawa, war clouds were gathering in Europe, in March Hitler seized Austria and his next victim was Czechoslovakia, the Munich crisis festered and came to a peak at the beginning of October. In Toronto relief, welfare and unemployment were high on the agenda of City Council. Salsberg's motions involved attempting to stop the TTC's effort to eliminate two-man cars; he urged the option of emergency measures by the federal government to provide relief work; he moved to relieve smaller rooming houses of tax assessment; complained of fraud in coal delivery; complained of the gas company charges for monthly meter service; protested the exemption from local taxes of the Royal York Hotel and urged reform of the City Hall's financing.

Motions on some of the issues were introduced by his Party colleague Stewart Smith and seconded by him or vice-versa. In his 1943 tenure he would occasionally second a motion proposed by

Lewis Duncan who was also a constant gadfly to the City Hall establishment. This, be it remembered, was the City Hall in whose administration the Orange Order reigned supreme, a City Hall of the 1920s and 1930s where minorities were rarely hired.

The outbreak of war, the Soviet-German non-aggression pact, the ambivalent Party position on these two issues and the outlawing of the Party put a stop to all further political candidacies for the next few years. The story of Joe's activities and whereabouts in the following few years has not yet been told. But after the German attack on the Soviet Union he, along with others who were in hiding in the early years of the war when the Party was outlawed under the War Measures Act, presented themselves to the authorities. Soon he was back in action, urging greater compliance with the war effort, urging higher industrial production and pressing for a second front.

On New Year's day 1943 he was once more elected alderman for Ward Four. This encouraged him to contest the provincial seat of St. Andrew and in the summer of 1943 he won in a four-way contest and was re-elected in 1945, 1948 and 1951.

Salsberg's election to the Legislature in the summer of 1943 was a signal for mass jubilation in Ward Four South. On the evening of the victory at the corner of College and Brunswick, a spontaneous parade formed itself and soon a column of several hundred were marching eastward towards Spadina with Joe Salsberg at its head. It was a warm August night. People were sitting outside trying to keep cool. They applauded the parade as it passed and many joined it. As the parade proceeded down Spadina someone shouted, "Joe's parents live nearby!" and, unknown to Joe, several hundred broke off from the main procession and turned left on Cecil Street to number 59 where they greeted the elder Salsbergs. First Abraham came out and said, "Thank you all for coming," and deferred to his wife who, he said, would address them. Sarah-Gittel spoke then saying: "May the Lord bless you all and may you derive as much satisfaction and pleasure from your children as I do from mine."

Salsberg's tenure in the Ontario Legislature lasted twelve years. He outlasted his colleague and party leader A. A. MacLeod, the

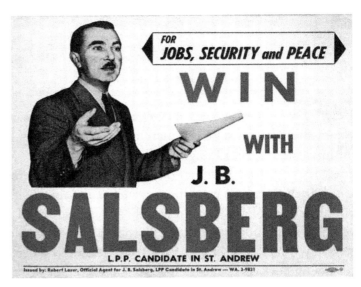

Salsberg used the slogan "Make the Rich Pay" in the Depression-era municipal election of 1935, as evidenced by the campaign button at left. Poster used during the provincial election of 1943 conveys a promise of "jobs, security and peace."

member for Bellwoods, by four years, the latter going down to defeat in 1951.

Salsberg was very much at home in the Legislature. The formal style of debate (all members being "honourable"), the civil level of argumentation, broken only occasionally by crude brawling, was admirably suited to his temperament, giving him a new status as a public tribune in his fight for the underdog and enabling him to indulge his penchant for rhetoric and repartee. He had greater opportunity to be of direct service to constituents. The ambience was broader—true, it was a provincial legislature, but the drama of democracy was played out in its chambers, with three parties vying for place and his own Party standing on the periphery—and he was good at pointing out the gaps and inadequacies.

One of Salsberg's first moves in the Legislature in 1944 was to propose an amendment to the government's anti-discrimination bill. The bill had a narrow area of jurisdiction, dealing only with discriminatory signs and placards. His amendment was to broaden the law's scope and outlaw discrimination in jobs. It was not until 1951 that the government introduced such legislation. In Canada in 1944, though a war was being fought against a racist power, there was still active discrimination against racial and religious minorities.

The Hansard index shows a wide scope of entries under Salsberg's name for the session of 1945. The headings under his name are:

family allowances; urges select committee on labour; urges lower voting age; discrimination at Hydro; vote of confidence on schools policy; eight firms violate labour laws; introduces anti-discrimination bill.

The following are some of the headings under his name in 1946:

exchange with Attorney General Blackwell on penal institutions; answers Drew on Communist charges; advocates jobs not Socialism; seeks assurances on Reform department; 40 hour bill defeated; urges labour code; would like seat on art committee; proposes low cost housing loans; charges Tories anti-labour; resents not having party status; attacks Drew for blocking social legislation.

Ralph Scane is a professor of law at the University of Toronto. When he was an undergraduate at the same institution he would cross the campus occasionally to listen to the debates at Queen's Park. He recalls that Salsberg and Macleod—especially Salsberg— were the most effective speakers in the House, especially at question time. "Their needling tactic was masterful. You had to admire it quite regardless of whether you agreed with their positions or not," says Scane today.

Another witness of those days is Sam Crystal, now public relations director for The Oshawa Group, but in those days a reporter for the old *Telegram*, assigned to the Legislature. When word reached the reporters that Salsberg was due to address the chamber the entire press gallery would rush to take their seats not to miss any of the sparkling exchange.

On the initiative, it is said, of Premier Leslie Frost an area in Northern Ontario beyond Fort Frances bears the name of Salsberg Township.

Salsberg often clashed with the members whether Liberal, Conservative or CCF but at all times maintained friendly relations with them. On one occasion after a lengthy debate on the establishment of Metropolitan Toronto in March 1953 he said:

Salsberg was considered one of the top debaters and orators in the provincial Parliament and observers of every political stripe would come to hear him. His political friends were many. Left, Salsberg with David Lewis, leader of the federal NDP, ca 1960s. Right, with Mayor Phillip Givens, ca 1960s.

"When I argue with the government or with honourable members it is not a personal battle, it is a battle over principles, over important issues. Sometimes in the heat of battle things are said and words are uttered which upon reflection, I'm sure, everybody feels could have been phrased differently or kept to oneself. However, I feel that it is human, and as far as I'm concerned, I assure all those who may have participated and got a little 'kick' out of heckling, I do not hold it against them at all."

Was the famous—many would say ill-advised—eulogy on Stalin he delivered in the Legislature on March 6, 1953 responsible for Salsberg's defeat at the polls two years later? No one, of course, can give a definitive answer. It is possible that, times being what they were, the growing distrust of Communism, the peaking of Cold War antagonisms and the demographic changes taking place in St. Andrew riding would have brought about defeat without its aid. Sam Lipshitz, who directed most of Salsberg's election campaigns, looks back at it decades later and does attribute considerable electoral importance to it. Sam says the Party applied severe pressure to have him deliver it. The argument ran: Salsberg was the only Communist parliamentarian in the British Commonwealth and it was his bounden duty to make the speech. By then Salsberg was no longer in the political bureau (roughly the cabinet) of the Party, from which he had been removed in 1952 because of his constant questioning about the fate of the Soviet Jewish writers. But he was still a central committee member and was seen as subject to party discipline and in the end he reluctantly agreed. In the 1955 campaign his Conservative opponent Allan Grossman, as might be expected and as was legitimate, made the most of it. The speech was reprinted and widely distributed in the riding.

Salsberg was always well regarded by his *landsleit* from Lagow, many of whom were among his warmest admirers, regardless of their political or religious affiliations. When he was elected to the Legislature they felt it inappropriate that an elected representative should lack adequate facilities to get about to visit his constituents and perform his various parliamentary duties. They raised the necessary funds and presented him with a Lincoln automobile. It being wartime, this was no current model but they sought out the most recent product.

The stories about Salsberg's close relations with his constituents are proverbial: the crowds that thronged his office on College Street, the assistance given the Chassidic rebbe freezing in his home because his oil furnace had been seized for non-payment of an installment, the open-ballot vote at which the venerable voter had one answer to all the routine questions put to him by the DRO such as "Your name?", "Your address?", "Your age?" that answer being the one word: "Zaltsberg!" All these stories have passed into the public domain.

The period of 1956 to 1959 was filled with the stormy struggle within the Party in general and within the United Jewish People's Order (UJPO) in particular. The revelations by Khrushchev at the Twentieth Party Congress had shocked many loyal Party members, shaken them out of a torpor and awakened them to certain grim realities. The worst fate imaginable for the Soviet Jewish writers had been confirmed beyond the most pessimistic scenarios and cynical predictions (the news came not from Khrushchev's revelations but

Left, with David Ben-Gurion in Israel. Right, at the Western Wall, Jerusalem.

from a different source). The disclosures established beyond any doubt that innocent people had been condemned, banished and imprisoned over a period of decades for no reason, that Stalin's axe had fallen capriciously on friend and foe alike, that the worst suspicions spread by the "East Broadway" Yiddish press could not begin to approximate the ugly truths that were now leaking out of the Soviet Union. The "Fatherland of the Workers" was seen indeed as a house of bondage, a cruel fraud. A growing number of Jewish Communists in Toronto who had automatically accepted the twists and turns of Soviet Communist policy could no longer brook the Machiavellian betrayals and tergiversations of "democratic centralism."

After an internecine battle that lasted three years they moved to separate from the UJPO and establish their own organization, the New Fraternal Jewish Association (NFJA), with a membership of less than 200. Despite the warnings of sympathizers that it would not last, it has shown remarkable longevity and is carrying on expanded programs to this day. Its founders included Morris Biderman, Paul Kerzner, Sam Lipshitz, Al Hershkovitz, Harry Binder and others. Joe Salsberg's own battle was fought not within the UJPO so much as within the Party but when he and the Party parted company he became very much part of the NFJA, serving as its president for a number of terms.

It was within this stormy and difficult period, in 1959, that his beloved life partner Dora prematurely passed away, a leading and important communal and social welfare figure in her own right. From that point on he was alone, though continuing to work with myriads of associates and friends.

This is not the occasion to tell the story of the separation of the New Fraternals, as they came to be called, from the UJPO. What can be said, however, is that it is a story unique to Toronto. While there are many Jewish Communists in the United States, France, Great Britain and Latin America whose disillusionment led them out of the Party, they remained on the sidelines or in a negative kind of limbo. Only in Toronto did the individuals realign themselves into a collective and form an active, viable association.

The story of Joe Salsberg's own estrangement from the Party and movement has been chronicled in various writings—most directly by Joe himself in the famous series of six installments in the *Vochenblatt* from October 25 to December 13, 1956, appearing in English and Yiddish. The series was reprinted around the world in Argentina, Uruguay, Paris and Tel Aviv. It charged the Soviet leadership with anti-Semitism, with choking off Jewish culture, and demanded a revision in its policies. He started with his suspicions, beginning in the late 1930s, of a change in policy, of the closing down of Jewish schools and cultural facilities. He told of his visit to the Soviet Union in 1939 which confirmed many of his doubts; but as a disciplined party member he made no public outcry, hoping for a change. After 1941 the war and the need to affirm solidarity in the desperate fight against Nazism and Fascism, put a damper on such discussion. The fears flared up again in the late 1940s and were not really alleviated by the Soviets' early recognition of Israel.

After his defeat in the elections of 1955 Salsberg travelled to the USSR and made another trip in 1956 as part of a Canadian Party deputation which met directly with Khrushchev. Khrushchev's parting comment to him was "not to be taken in by the Baruchs." This puzzled Salsberg until he remembered that Khrushchev had before him his own curriculum vitae where his name in full was given as Joseph Baruch Salsberg, which enabled Khrushchev to make the allusion to the noted American capitalist.

The period from 1959 to the present has been a period of rebuilding confidences, a period of restoration, recovery and revival for Joseph Salsberg. His interests have been unchanged: the working man and woman; the Jewish community and the need for democracy in its leadership; the cultural world of Yiddish letters; social welfare and social security; a humane society. These issues have been played on a different stage with a different cast of characters. The circumstances are, of course, altered: the world of Spadina and College is no more, the needle trades no longer employ a Jewish labour force of thousands, upward mobility has transformed the face of the Jewish community. But the issues are not all that different: medical care for all; laissez-faire (now called "privatization") or a mixed economy; war or peace—not always as black and white as it seemed. There are new issues to be argued: the problem of Quebec and its separation, the continuing question of the future of Soviet Jewry, even under the new and radically changed circumstances; doves vs. hawks in Israel. Joe has something to contribute to all.

Joseph Salsberg's interests in the past thirty years cut across the entire spectrum of the community, the Jewish and national agenda. He has been an active participant in the affairs of the Canadian Jewish Congress as a member of its national executive committee and its Ontario regional executive. He has been national chairman of the cjc's committee for Yiddish. He has received the cjc's Samuel Bronfman Medal. In the Ontario region he held simultaneously the two portfolios of Soviet Jewry and the Committee for Yiddish, and was also the first chairman to be named for each. A staunch opponent of the plan to merge Congress with the Welfare Fund, he was asked when the first partial merger took place, "What will you do now?" He answered, "Learn to live under water."

He is an officer and honourary vice-president of the Jewish Federation of Greater Toronto (JFGT) recently renamed from Toronto Jewish Congress and before that known as the United Jewish Welfare Fund. This agency has also conferred upon him

94

the Ben Sadowski Award. The portfolio of Soviet Jewry, when he took it on, and for a long time afterwards was one of constant action and movement: mass demonstrations as Kosygin moved across the country, rallies, protests, deputations, Simchat Torah events, coordination with Women for Soviet Jewry, with student groups, with the Group of 35, letter-writing campaigns, etcetera, all through the 1970s and 1980s. It was clearly not a letterhead sinecure but a task requiring constant attention, planning and follow-up.

In his own organization, the New Fraternal, he has served as president for a number of terms. He is chairman of the editorial board that publishes *Fraternally Yours*, a well-edited bilingual periodical that is far more than a house organ. The NFJA carries on a year-round program of lectures, social and cultural events and fund-raising and maintains the J. B. Salsberg Medical Clinic in Kiryat Yam, Israel.

Joe Salsberg as an octogenarian (*ben shmonim le'g'vurah* says the old Jewish adage, eighty is for strength) has been available as speaker for the UJA and in the province for UIA, carrying the word as far afield as Thunder Bay and Sault Ste. Marie. The same applies to the Histadrut–Bikur Cholim. He has addressed *landsmanshaften* and B'nai Brith lodges and has gotten a particular satisfaction from speaking to groups of Moroccan Jews—brethren from another cultural milieu.

B'nai Brith in Ontario named him their chairman for Soviet Jewry programs and activities. He is an officer of the Jewish Family and Child Service. But his most public and visible persona has been one which has put him in unmediated contact with a public he may not otherwise have met in such a direct fashion. This has been his weekly column of comment in the *Canadian Jewish News*. Here he can reach thousands of readers who reach for him first on opening the weekly. His subject matter embraces the worlds of universalism and particularism; labour and capital; religion and state here and in Israel; the kibbutzim and their fate; Israel among the nations; the news from Moscow under its changing leaderships; the nostalgic memories of studying *Peyrek* (*Ethics of the Fathers*) in the summer outdoors in Lagow; Spadina of old and its many-sided Jewish kaleidoscope; the Kirshenbaum, Grafstein and Ladowsky families; his contemporaries as they pass from the scene—all embellished with the wisdom and discretion of his Uncle Eliezer.

Joe's personality has been such that he found no difficulty in turning enemies into staunch friends. He had no firmer political foe on the Canadian political scene than NDP–CCF leader David Lewis. In 1972 David Lewis was chairman of Joe's seventieth birthday dinner. Another longtime antagonist was fur worker unionist Max Federman whose factions had engaged in physical battles with the colleagues and followers of Joe Salsberg. Recently I spoke to Max in the course of preparing this piece, asking for an interview on his relations and experience with Joe. Max responded with keen enthusiasm. Unfortunately, it was only weeks before Max's passing and the interview couldn't be held. Another former political adversary, Harry Simon, fortunately was interviewed and despite their past disagreements and frictions, spoke about him with friendliness and warmth.

Much the same applies to the "bourgeois" parties. In 1955 Tory Premier Leslie Frost said: "For three and a half years the Liberals sat in Legislature with no policy at all. Anything constructive they left for a single member of a socialist party to advance—J.B. Salsberg." Journalist and broadcaster Gordon Sinclair was a known enthusiastic support of capitalism. Speaking on CFRB in 1955, he said: "Salsberg, by all admission was one of the best debaters in the house."

Joe Salsberg has had not one but numerous careers—Labour Zionist executive, union organizer, Communist Party strategist, alderman, parliamentarian, journalist and in the last thirty years, activist in many causes of a constructive and positive nature: Israel and her security; the integrity and the viability of the Jewish people wherever they live, including the lands of the former Soviet Union. His name is remembered and will continue to be remembered wherever Jews congregate to celebrate the future or record the past. ❦

Undated photograph of Ben Kayfetz at his desk at 150 Beverley Street.

Looking Back at the Beverley Street Era

MY OWN DIRECT INVOLVEMENT with Canadian Jewish Congress dates from early 1947 when I returned from a postwar stint with Control Commission for Germany and joined the CJC staff. I was thirty years old and glad to get the $60-a-week job as director of public relations for its Ontario region.

It was one year and ten months after the end of World War Two, there was no such thing as a state of Israel, and 150 Beverley Street was still planted firmly in the middle of a solidly Jewish-settled area, surrounded and beset by Jewish institutions of every shape and kind. Up the street was Scheuer House, Murray House, the Apter Centre, the Workmen's Circle. Across the road was the Eitz Chaim Talmud Torah, around the corner the Stashover Shul, and Cecil Street, two blocks away, just swarmed with institutions: the Folks Farein, the Poilisher Shul, the Jewish Old Folks Home (as it was plainly and unpretentiously named), the Farband, the Strettener Rebbe, the Chevra Shass, and others. And on Huron Street there stood a hovel that gloried in the name Anshei New York!

Shortly after I started, though the war had been over for almost two years, austerity rules set in that had never existed during the war

From "Old Days at building on 150 Beverley are recalled," Canadian Jewish News, Sept, 15, 1983. With additions from an article in the Congress Bulletin.

itself. Restaurants were forbidden to serve meat on Tuesdays. For some time, perhaps a year, we had meatless Tuesdays. On Tuesdays we hied ourselves over to the Belvedere on Bay and Dundas, which served spaghetti in ten different versions, styles and sauces.

Chinatown in those days ended sharply at University Avenue and there were two major synagogues downtown: one on University Avenue on the present site of Bell Canada and the other on McCaul Street on the present site of Silver's car park. And on Dundas Street from St. Patrick to Simcoe, where the police station now stands, was Goldberg's Monuments where seventeen years before, in 1930, a murder had taken place for which, for the first time in Toronto, a Jew had been hanged. On the north side of the same block, on the site of the present "Number One Park Lane" complex, stood Dow's Brewery. On the south side of Dundas just east of McCaul was Solomon's Delicatessen, but if you just ordered a sandwich you'd be eyed queerly as an intruder, for it was in reality a front for a flourishing bookmaking operation with a backroom telephone constantly on the go. And next door to us was the RCMP billets—now the Italian Consulate.

So much for the outside ambience. The Congress took up the second floor of the old building known as Chudleigh House. The main floor was a catering house owned by Arnold Hundert who provided the Congress and its staff and committee members with the required sandwiches and assorted victuals both for formal committee meetings and informal snacks. Hundert was once a partner in the aptly named Eppes Essen kosher corned beef emporium on College and Brunswick. He lived on the premises with his wife, son, daughter, son-in-law and granddaughter.

Occasionally in my first two years I would drop into the office after hours, slipping in unobtrusively upstairs to check or revise some correspondence or to retrieve a letter or leaflet. There was generally a wedding or some *simcha* taking place on the main floor for Chudleigh House was still a favourite catering spot. Sometimes if the *simcha* was a stag I would hear Lou Jacobi's stag jokes and raunchy punchlines floating up from the festivities below. He told them with such great gusto. It was shortly after this that Jacobi left for London's West End where on short order he made a name for himself in the entertainment world.

The United Jewish Welfare Fund was still located in the Hermant Building at 21 Dundas Square; I believe it didn't move into the building on Beverley until about 1952. At campaign time it would move lock, stock and barrel into the King Edward Hotel where the campaign headquarters would be located. Staff would be corraled from the Congress and other agencies and the campaign would proceed.

Speaking of the King Edward, we were more attuned to having functions and meetings in hotels then. All national meetings of Congress and its various committees were held at the Royal York or King Eddie in Toronto and the Mount Royal in Montreal. Luncheons for visitors from the United States or Britain were in a private dining room at one of the two hotels. Why so? I'm not sure. For one thing total *kashrut* was not an indispensable requirement in that period. A fish plate was accepted as a replacement. Also, the prices at the hotels were within range and reason and had not yet taken flight as they did in later years.

When I began, the Jewish Immigrant Aid Society (JIAS) was still in the Tip Top building on Spadina and College, but at some point in the next year or so, when the immigrants started to roll in from the Displaced Persons camps, it moved directly across us to 147–149 Beverley, including the corner house on D'Arcy Street that carries the plaque certifying that "Mackenzie King slept here."

The nominal head of Congress at that time was Ben Sadowski, president of the region. In actual fact, the working head was Eddie Gelber, one of the many ardent volunteers who chaired countless committee meetings on behalf of Congress; I clearly recall Eddie Gelber chairing executive meetings but not Sadowski who was too preoccupied building the new hospital. I soon became familiar with the ringing phrase uttered repeatedly by Gelber—"the totality of Jewish life"—and I still hear it echoing down the decades. It summed up concisely the main concern of our CJC leaders to improve the quality of Jewish life, not only in our three regional community centres then in Montreal, Toronto and Winnipeg, but for Jewry around the world.

The director then was Sol Grand who was quite young, about twenty-six, but an alert, aggressive and gifted individual. He was raised in Saskatchewan and had attended university in that province and in Manitoba. There had been some campus controversy he was involved in in Saskatchewan (student rebellion has been a fixture long before the events of the 1960s) though I never learned the details, and he had moved on to Winnipeg. I got along well with Sol but he did have a rather irascible temper and from time to time I would hear loud, violent noises coming out of his office (the one Stephen Speisman is in now) and then I'd see Freda Green or Ruth Cohen emerge in a torrent of tears. Once I saw Shmuel Mayer Shapiro, editor of the *Hebrew Journal*, storm out after one of these screaming sessions. But oddly enough, Sol never seemed to pick one of his thunderous altercations with *balebatim* like Ben Sadowski or Irving Oelbaum; though I believe he did once with Gurston Allen who was then quite active both in Congress and the Welfare Fund.

The following year Sol was persuaded by Ben Sadowski to take over the directorship of the new Mount Sinai Hospital then being built on University Avenue. (He had worked with the United Jewish Welfare Fund before coming to Congress and had had fundraising experience.) Tragically, he died quite suddenly on New Year's Eve several years later leaving his widow Elaine Grand who was one of the interviewing personalities in the early days of CBC television.

Before Sol left he hired a new staff member, Daniel Drutz, who had just completed a course at the School of Social Work after leaving the Air Force. By the time Drutz came in Sol's successor Ben Lappin was on the scene. Ben was no stranger to Congress, having worked there before from 1942 to 1946 as executive secretary of the Joint Public Relations Committee and having left to take a course at the university. Ben Lappin served ten years from 1948 to 1958, which were years of great hustle and bustle, years of great achievement, the mass influx of immigrants, the reorganization of the United Jewish Relief Agency (UJRA) to cope with this influx, the enactment of the Fair Employment (anti-discrimination) laws, the setting up of Congress's regular school visits in the region.

In 1958 Ben Lappin embarked on an academic career and became head of the School of Social Work of Bar Ilan University. He was replaced at Congress by Myer Sharzer, a newspaperman from Winnipeg who had "gone wrong" and entered the Jewish communal service. He stayed fourteen years until his sudden passing in 1972.

Prior to the period when I came to Congress there had been a number of executive directors: Martin Cohn, Ethel Ostry, Maurice Gold, Oscar Cohen (now retired from the Anti-Defamation League of B'nai Brith), Sam Abramson (now in retirement directing his time between New York and the Heritage Commission of World Jewish Congress), the late Moses Z. Frank (who was a noted Hebrew essayist as well as an English and Yiddish journalist). The very first executive secretary of Congress in Ontario is still among us—he is Alexander Brown who went on to a career in Jewish education. He can tell some serio-comic stories about the salaries Congress paid in those Depression-ridden days.

We were fortunate in the late 1940s to know the inimitable H. M. Caiserman, the man who was so instrumental in getting Congress off the ground initially in 1919 and again in its second incarnation in 1934. He would come from Montreal twice a year, once in the early pre-Passover spring to conduct the *Moess Chittin* campaign and once again in the early fall to carry out the Yizkor campaign. This was before the Israel Bond campaign was established and the Yizkor fund had clear sailing in the synagogues on Atonement Day.

Hanania Caiserman was already in his sixties but abounding with drive and enthusiasm. He would on occasion share his reminiscences with us junior staffers, when as a boy from Roumania making his way across the face of Europe he would hawk the *Avanti* daily in Milan. (It was Mussolini's socialist newspaper before he became the fascist *Duce*.) He would work furiously in his office and produce Yiddish reviews and commentaries which he would send off in all directions to papers in Uruguay, Argentina, France and

101

Israel. He would indite gallant and courtly love poems in English to women guests at the King Edward Hotel, where he stayed. (I picked up one of these on the floor in the office once. To my eternal regret I did not keep it.)

He startled me once by asking me—of all people—for the correct spelling of basic Hebrew words often used in Yiddish like *mitzvah, ganeff,* etcetera—he a lifelong Yiddish writer. Caiserman, a colourful lively personality, was a link with the older and earlier Congress—when people thought in terms of the elite and the masses, the uptown and the downtown, terms which were a more direct reflection of the community's make-up and self-perception than today.

It was that tense pre-State period between 1945 and 1948, in the uneasy final years of the British Mandate in Palestine when mass arrests and imprisonments, ambushes, boycotts, blockades, bombings and hangings were tearing apart the peace of the Middle East and when Jews felt a great disillusionment after the initial postwar feeling of liberation. The Labour government in Great Britain which while in Opposition had sworn to promote Jewish settlement was now violently suppressing it, jailing such moderate Zionist leaders as Moshe Shertok and David Ben Gurion. Jews everywhere were tense and worried. The Haganah and the Irgun each had their protagonists in the Diaspora community, the local press was hostile, blaming the *yishuv* as a whole for the acts of the terrorists. Ontario was a very British-minded province and the Jews were perceived by many (and by themselves in part as well) as being aligned against the British on the Palestine issue.

I recall going to the old editorial offices of the *Telegram* on Bay and Melinda in the company of Sam Zacks, Eddie Gelber and Irving Oelbaum to protest a hostile editorial. We brought with us Nathan Phillips, then still an alderman but someone who was *persona grata* with such a Tory institution as the *Telegram*. What I recall most about that meeting in the office of editor C. O. Knowles was a good-natured wrist and body-wrestling contest that went on between Nate Phillips and Knowles, a preliminary warming-

Left, Hananiah Meyer Caiserman was general secretary of Canadian Jewish Congress from 1919 to 1950. Right, Nathan Phillips, lawyer, alderman and future mayor, Toronto 1930.

up ritual that threatened to develop into a major grappling bout between the two venerable but informal personalities both white-thatched at the time. It was, as I recall, a rather incongruous sight.

What did Congress provide and what were its concerns back then? Well, the Joint Public Relations Committee, a joint activity with B'nai Brith, was a going concern. This was the job I had taken on; the name was later changed to Joint Community Relations. Chairman for Ontario was Rabbi Abraham Feinberg of Holy Blossom Temple. There was an arbitration chairman whose task it was to settle disputes of a communal component. Research, adult education, and refugee case work (handled by Edna Keller) were other major concerns. There was also a Societies Division that brought together the *landsmanshaften*, the mutual benefit associations and the fraternal lodges, all of which constituted a sizable segment of our community. This represented what was called *di massen* ("the masses") by the orators and Congress philosophers such as Yiddish editor Shmuel Mayer Shapiro. Some of its chairmen were the late Carl Herlick, a lawyer, and the late Alfred Green, a gem merchant who came into Congress as a protege of Archie Bennett. Others involved were Karl Cohl, Sam Lent, Harry Mangel, Sam Traub and Morris Biderman.

There was a consistent tug-of-war with the leftists from the United Jewish Peoples Order who, as an opposition group, were constantly stirring up the fires of dissension. Congress had admitted them to membership in 1943 in the euphoria of the wartime alliance with the Soviet Union and they had representatives on most committees; on my committee they were Joshua Gershman and Joseph B. Salsberg.

By the end of 1947 the postwar period had finally begun in earnest and the United Nations, then still in Flushing Meadows in Queens, voted to partition Palestine and authorize a Jewish state. As 1947 rolled out and ran into 1948 it became clear what the major thrust of Congress was going to be for the next few years. By this time Ben Lappin had taken over the helm at the CJC and had begun organizing the facilities for the immigrant influx. First there were the orphans, called the project on European Youth; the first batch of European orphans had just arrived at Union Station. Then Congress, the clothing manufacturers and the needle trade unions jointly devised a plan to bring over tailors, then furriers, then millinery workers, recruiting them from the DP camps. The tailor plan was headed by Max Enkin, the furrier scheme by Joe Kerbel and Max Federman.

We intuited then that there had been a change of policy on the part of government. We realized that it was not necessarily a sudden case of philo-Semitism but that postwar Canada, if it meant to develop its resources, clearly needed manpower. It was not for another thirty-five years or so until the revelations of Troper and Abella in *None Is Too Many* that we learned how determined Ottawa had been until then to keep out the Jews.

The Jewish Immigrant Aid Society which worked closely with Congress did not then have a permanent director in its Toronto office. At one point it was Hy Latch who introduced me to a younger brother visiting from Montreal whose name was not Latch but Layton—Irving Layton, an up-and-coming poet (both were born Lazarovitch in Roumania). Latch left and was followed by a pharmacist–social worker named Bill Greenberg and afterwards by Montreal social worker Matthew Ram. Mannie Kraicer, the former director, returned from Germany where he was on loan to the United Nations Relief and Rehabilitation Administration but after a while he left for the new State of Israel where he worked for HIAS International. As a consequence Congress was thrown into immigration work to a greater extent than otherwise would have been the case.

Danny Drutz arrived in time to cope with the heavy influx of newcomers, their problems of housing, jobs, subsistence (this was then handled by the UJRA)—all of which prepared him to take the JIAS directorship in 1950. And Carl Rossi's first task on the community scene was to handle the clothing depot for the immigrants.

Who were then the Congress staff? Freda Green (nee Gussen) did research—I believe though I wasn't sure, as she left shortly after. Ruth Cohen handled publicity and press matters. She was quite young, twenty-three or twenty-four at the time. Murray Shiff did education, youth and societies, though the coming fall he went to Chicago where Congress staked him to a BA course at the University of Chicago, which he did in two years, returning in 1949.

And there were three persons doing part-time work in public relations, as we then termed community relations: Bill Solkin, a social work student, Fred Biderman, a Montrealer who shortly thereafter went on *aliyah*, and Sidney Wax, a medical student (now Dr. Wax) who was doing a research project related to the movie *Gentleman's Agreement* that had just come out.

My secretary was Freda Levine, then all of seventeen but already married and showing an amazing precocity and maturity. Today she's an advisor to Bob Kaplan, the Solicitor General, and if he keeps going wrong it's likely because he isn't following her advice.

The staff, as you see, was much smaller then, but so was the program. There was no Orthodox division or *kashrut* department, and the chaplaincy program had not yet been established. There was no Archives program, no field worker for the region, no travelling education supervisor for the Jewish schools in the region

(Joseph Klinghofer had not yet arrived in Canada). Nor was there a Committee for Yiddish; perhaps the future of Yiddish seemed secure enough not to need a committee. The idea of a Soviet Jewry program for Jews wanting out of the Soviet Union lay far far ahead in the future; if anyone had suggested there'd be a move on their part to leave Russia for Palestine, he'd have been dismissed as mad. For obvious reasons there was not yet any need for a Committee for Jews in Arab Lands or for Ethiopian Jews. In fact, looking back at it from the present point of view it was pretty Utopian in a strangely paradoxical way, since all this *tzores* had not yet been felt—although the Holocaust, only two years behind us, lay fairly heavy on our consciousness.

The most vulnerable job, the one with the highest mortality rate, was for many years the publicity director of the United Jewish Appeal. The first one to hold the post for some length of time was Phil Stone, followed by Morris Lucow and Esther Mehr and Bob Gottlieb. But before Phil Stone's time the fatality rate was high— very high—in one case a mere two weeks: not all were fired, some were lured away by better offers. Their names included Gordon Allen, Lou Frydhandler, Irving Herman, Ed Magder, Leo Moss (who went to the Labour Zionist Movement), Marvin Needelman, Chaim Newman, Jack Orenstein (who went to Shaarei Shomayim, later to Beth Tzedec), Mort Schlossman, Earl Ivan Shaffer, Lester Sugarman (who went to Holy Blossom, later to CBC) and Len Weingrad.

Who were some of the lay leaders of that day? There was the incomparable Sam Kronick who virtually lived at 150 Beverley Street which served as his second home. A sofa was brought in for him so he could catch forty winks or stretch out when he was tired. He was chairman of the UJRA and conducted his own private welfare and distribution agency carrying on the tradition of one-on-one charity. He had nothing but disdain for the new-fangled notions of the trained social worker. But could such individuals dispensing of welfare allow the cheat to prosper? He acknowledged this, responding that it was better for a hundred frauds to prosper, so long as one needy supplicant was provided. Sam, thinking of his own former days as a *g'veer*, had a favourite Hebrew expression which reflected the cynical attitude of society: *Oni choshuv k'mesa*, which translated both literally and loosely meant: "A pauper has the value of a corpse."

Dr. Sam Hurwich was a popular and esteemed figure in the Jewish community, and one of his communal homes (he had a number of them) was the Congress. Born in Toronto, he was at home in English, Yiddish and Hebrew, and his words in all three languages were listened to with deference and attention. A Labour Zionist, he fulfilled the tenets of his ideology to work for Zion and to build a strong Jewish community in the Diaspora. His wife, Rivka, paralleled his communal career in every way.

Irving Oelbaum became Ontario region president in 1949 and directed the affairs of the region for a number of years. He was already very much immersed in Congress activity, having been a national chairman of public relations (as community relations was then termed). For a time Oelbaum held the regional chairman's gavel; he eventually handed it to Professor Jacob Finkelman who in turn passed it to Meyer W. Gasner. A New Yorker who had been successfully transplanted to Canada, Gasner served a lengthy term through most of the 1960s.

When I was engaged for my job, I was interviewed separately by two people, Oelbaum and Rabbi Abraham Feinberg. This was before the days of curricula vitae or of "search committees." In April 1947 Oelbaum was only forty-seven but his shock of prematurely white hair belied his age and lent him a grandfatherly appearance, which only served to enhance his image as a "father figure." He and his brothers owned and managed a large paper bag and products factory and had other business interests. But he never let these interfere with community work. He would rise every day before dawn and be at his office at five o'clock each morning. This enabled him to complete the day's commercial business by 10 A.M., making it possible to devote the rest of the day to community matters. On my own committee, the JPRC, he always defied identification, and both Congress and

B'nai Brith would list him as their particular nominee.

Who were some rabbis active then in Congress? Rabbi Feinberg, the former radio singer and the son of an impoverished cantor in Ohio, was chairman of the Public Relations Committee. He was wont to come out with public statements from time to time that would raise a few hackles in some circles of the community (including Congress). Once it was a question about the propriety of Christmas carols in the public schools. It almost brought the roof down, the reaction even including a counter-statement from the bearded Rabbi Price. Another time, Feinberg denounced the Canadian government for discriminating against Jewish nurses in its immigration procedures. This was denied all round, but current information seems to bear out his charges.

Rabbi Abraham Kelman left Toronto for Brooklyn in 1950. Before that, he was helpful in many Congress endeavors. In those days, Abraham Aaron Price and David Ochs, both traditional rabbonim with patriarchal beards, vied for the spiritual leadership of the Orthodox community.

These are some random recollections summoned up from memory of the events of those early postwar years of 1947, 1948 and 1949. The community was in a state of transition from the Depression and wartime years to the ease, tranquility and prosperity of the 1950s. But in the period of which I write, though the war was over, the 1950s had not yet arrived. The battles and blockades that heralded the Jewish state were still being fought. The very idea of an independent Jewish republic—not a colony, not a mandated possession—seemed difficult to conceptualize. The survivors of the death camps who had lived through unbelievable experiences with tattoed wrists and blighted years of hell on earth were arriving on these shores to begin life anew.

I could go on writing about Congress personalities I have admired for many more pages. I've put these reminiscences together as a sentimental memento on the occasion of our leaving the Beverley Street locale, a spot that has housed and contained the working centre of our community for the past fifty years. ❧

Hospitals enforced strict quotas against Jews in the early days. Toronto General Hospital in its new home, College Street east of University Avenue, 1913.

Only Yesterday: From Discrimination to Acceptance

THIS EVENING I want to say something about the developments in our community that have taken place in its occupational structure and vocational pattern and in its general state of co-existence with the larger community. I am not an economist and have no training in that science and what I have to say is not based on statistical data; no input of computered figures has been placed into the maw of the IBM machine. This is not to belittle the value of statistics. It is only that they have not been collected or if they do exist somewhere in a raw state I have had no access to them. I will be relying only on my purely personal observations sometimes as an insider, sometimes as a casual observer from the outside assessing the advantages and liabilities of both. Why do I say "only yesterday?" I am dealing with a situation that existed right up to the end of World War Two and for some period after. Twenty-seven years is a sizable slice of time but to me it still seems like only yesterday. Yet so much has elapsed and the changes are so startling in some respects.

Delivered to the Toronto Jewish Historical Society, May, 1972.

View from University & Dundas, 1930, shows Goel Tzedec at lower right, Armouries, City Hall, Eaton factories, unfinished

Let's take the teaching profession. There were in Toronto small numbers of Jewish teachers in the public schools, even smaller numbers in the high schools. It was generally accepted that Jewish high school teachers had to go into *golus* (exile) be it in Fort William, Barrie or Galt or Owen Sound before they were permitted to enter the charmed circle of teaching in Toronto—if indeed they were so fortunate. Some spent years—decades—in this *golus* servitude. Some never left it. Most in fact never broke out of *golus* if they stayed in teaching. In my own case, and this was a field I had studied for at one point (it was in 1941), I was engaged at a private boys school in Niagara Falls where the headmaster (and owner of the school for it was a private enterprise venture) who was a fearless, freethinking nineteenth-century liberal, suggested to me that it would be better all round if I passed as a Czechoslovak. He didn't even have the excuse of religious bigotry to explain his proposal for he was an agnostic. And what the special *yichus* was about being Czechoslovak in preference to being Jewish, I failed to see then or now. I don't know what he told others but I never had the embarrassment of being addressed in Czech or Slovak by any chance visitor as I never followed his suggestion. So rare were Jewish teachers and so little knowledge was there about Jews in general that when we once had a redheaded Jewish student teacher from the Ontario College of Education take our class at Parkdale Collegiate where I was a student in the first half of the 1930s, a boy

110

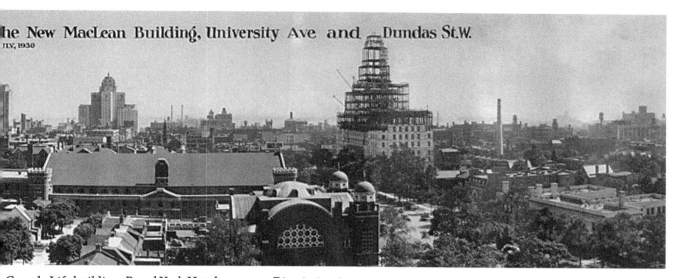

Canada Life building, Royal York Hotel, etcetera. Discrimination against minorities was both prevalent and legal back then.

next to me named Macdonald whispered in my ear that this student teacher obviously must have had his hair dyed. After all everyone knows that Jews never have red hair naturally!

At the University—there was only one in Toronto in the second half of the 1930s when I attended as a student—I only knew of two Jews on the faculty. There was Jacob Finkelman who lectured to me in law and whom I got to know years later in the Canadian Jewish Congress. He was then a young man of twenty-seven but seemed to me to be a man of vast age and maturity. And there was a Jewish woman in mathematics who did not rise beyond a junior rank of lecturer as she bore a double liability—her sex and her religion. The situation in the United States was no better. A few decades earlier Ludwig Lewisohn found that while he was permitted to lecture in German literature, English literature was reserved for the Anglo-Saxons. He had to wait until the formation of Brandeis University in his old age before he fulfilled his lifelong ambition.

I recall asking a younger member of the staff in the department where I was enrolled as an undergraduate—I was toying with the idea of going into the field academically—and he responded by discouraging me. Not because I was not likely to qualify or didn't have the goods (though that might have been accurate) but because Jews simply could not expect to get appointments here or in the States—he himself was an American and he knew the situation in that country.

111

Let's now turn to engineering. A few years ago while on my rounds in the Ontario region I spoke to a merchant—he was a jeweler—in one of the small Ontario cities. He was then in his mid-fifties. In the chat it emerged that he was a graduate engineer from the University of Toronto having completed his course in the 1930s. He didn't stay in the profession as it was clearly no place for a Jewish boy in those days. In another case I know of a man closer to me in age who graduated in engineering and who wound up in the *shmattah* business. Dependent as engineers were on employment by others and with the added liability of a Depression with very little construction going on, they drifted into other occupations. About all of these I am somewhat at a serious disadvantage as there are in this audience, I'm sure, persons who are much more familiar with the story in any given profession and who can provide more accurate and more reliable facts. However, please remember I am only giving a personal, impressionistic story, not an exhaustive authoritative documentation. I feel this particularly so in the next area I'll be dealing with, that of medicine.

Here, happily, the area has been covered by two eminent men who have written books telling their own story of the uphill struggle that was fought in medicine for the proper recognition of the Jewish medical man. In Toronto the book is *A Doctor's Memoir*, by Abe Willinsky, and in Montreal it is *Small Patients*, the life story of the late Alton Goldbloom, one of the country's pioneer pediatricians. Willinsky once had to pass for Greek Orthodox because I suppose his Slavic sounding name made it plausible though (as in my own case) I fail to see its *yichus* over against a Jewish identity. From 1929 the Toronto General Hospital apparently adopted the practice of accepting one Jewish intern per year, a form of *numerus clausus* that they had no compunction about. The surgeon-in-chief of a leading Toronto civic-supported hospital was reported to have stated that Jewish doctors would be appointed to staff "over his dead body." The fact that these institutions were supported by taxes levied on all citizens irrespective of religious label was a detail that went quite unnoticed.

One point that should be cleared up on this question is the matter of admission to medical school. The impression is about in many quarters that the University of Toronto medical school has always had a quota system in admission. Not so. There was no problem about admission to the U of T medical school in the 1930s at any rate, provided the student had the qualifying matriculation credits. The problem arose at the end of the training process when the student graduated and sought a hospital that would accept him as an intern. And that is where we lost a great number of talented and bright young men and women who had to go to the United States for their internships. Some returned here but many—perhaps the majority—stayed away and became part of the brain drain. This is not to say that there was no discrimination against Jews in medicine in the United States. Actually it was worse there for there it occurred at the other end of the process, at the initial point, at admission when the student sought entry to medical school. We all know to this day of Jewish medical students from the States going as far afield as Italy.

And the severe competition for places in medical schools started much earlier than in Canada. In the early 1930s when admission to the medical schools in Canada, or at least in Toronto, was quite straightforward, the American Jews were facing all sorts of obstacles. The restrictions here started only during World War Two when as a wartime measure to expedite the supply of doctors, tuition fees were dropped at the U of T medical school on condition that the graduates go directly into the armed services. When this increased the number of applicants a system of restrictions, including an unofficial religious quota, was applied.

We live in a metropolis where the two major department stores "bestride the city like a colossus." Having been raised here, I was always accustomed to thinking of downtown Toronto as consisting of two major elements: Eaton's and Simpsons and whatever else sprung up between and beside these mammoth institutions. As far as their record of employment of Jews is concerned it was nothing to be proud of. To be sure when they conducted their own tailoring shops in the period before World War One the staff was almost exclusively Jewish—who else were tailors, finishers, bushelers in those days? I've even heard tell the story of the Jew who was dismissed because he came in to work on Yom Kippur—or was it the Sabbath?

The office and retail section, however, was a different story. In these was often repeated a rather strange account—a tale of enforced Marranos in the twentieth century. Jewish girls would take a job in the sales department and give their religion as some safe Protestant denomination. They would work for several months— until Doomsday or very appropriately and literally *Yom Ha-Din* or Yom Kippur in its more common name. She would be away that day and on her return would find a little yellow slip in her pay envelope informing her of her dismissal. Her absence on that day had identified her as Jewish—that was enough for her discharge.

Stepping into the political field for a moment, what were things like then? Well, Jews could get ahead in politics. There had been a Jewish alderman once in the 1880s, another named Louis Singer in 1912, and from the early 1920s almost continually a brace of Jewish aldermen—almost always lawyers—but always representing the old Ward Four, the area of Jewish settlement in the central part of the city. It was difficult for many years for a Jewish candidate to win in nearby Ward Five because the number of Jewish residents was not quite big enough. In other words Jews could rise in politics—but they had to get their start in a Jewish riding.

This applied across the country. In Montreal back in 1917 the Laurier regime designated Cartier as a "Jewish riding" and it was represented in turn by Sam Jacobs, Peter Bercovitch, Louis Fitch, Sam Rose, Leon Crestohl and Milton Klein until it disappeared in the redistribution. Likewise in Toronto West Centre or Spadina it was Sam Factor and David Croll and in Winnipeg North it was Abe Heaps. Now, there's nothing wrong with a Jewish MP or MPP representing a Jewish riding. But it's rather confining to have to start in some particular riding designated as Jewish—suppose you have an inclination or opportunity to run in another area? Until recently it wasn't done.

In the far-off days when Highway 2 was the only artery leading into Toronto from Hamilton on the west, one of the eyesores that greeted the traveller was a placard over a private beach just by the Humber River called Brookers. Brookers used to display a sign over their gate which read "Gentiles Only." At the other end of the city when in 1933 large numbers of Jews started to visit Kew Beach, squads of young hoodlums, inspired by what had happened in Germany earlier that year, banded together in a "Swastika Club" to intimidate the Jews, keeping them away from the eastern preserves of Toronto by strong-arm bullyboy methods. An entire body of mythology has grown up about these incidents and the Christie Pits skirmish that followed; in retrospect they've expanded in size and meaning, but they did occur, there was fisticuffs and trucks did marshal men at Spadina and Dundas to carry off the fighting forces to the landing shores of Operation Counterswastika in the East End.

Housing was clearly restricted. I didn't realize this in my innocence. I knew that the area from Bloor to Queen to University to Ossington was predominantly Jewish. I vaguely knew that out beyond this area there was a vast *terra incognita* inhabited mainly by Gentiles. What happened when Jews tried to rent or buy in these areas I never knew because the idea had certainly not occurred to me. It was brought to my attention on contact with refugees from Germany and Czechoslovakia who came to Canada in the late 1930s and from whom I heard that Jews couldn't live there. On one occasion a phrase of theirs caught me up short and shook me when one of them referred to a section of the city as "*wo Juden nicht durfen*"—where Jews aren't permitted. This had such a ring of repression in it that I wondered if we were living in the same city. The answer is that we were, but I had never ventured out of the area of my immediate environment—at least not to rent or buy. In 1941 the war was already on and I overheard my employer's wife phoning hour after hour in reply to advertisements. Each time she called she was looking for an apartment—she would ask as a matter of course, "Is it restricted?" I was somewhat taken aback.

She occasionally explained "We're Jewish" but most of the time the code word "restricted" was fully understood on the other side of the phone. I realized then—and even more so in retrospect—that this was a degrading, humiliating procedure to go through but go through with it she did.

In another case I know of, immediately after the war's end, a discharged medical corps captain, still in uniform, was negotiating for a purchase of a home in the Queensway area on the western side of Toronto. All was well until the would-be buyer mentioned, quite in passing, that he was Jewish. This destroyed the entire negotiation, the real estate agent explaining that he was bound by some unwritten agreement (or perhaps it was written) not to sell to Jews—even Jews who had just defended their country.

I have touched on teaching, the universities, engineering, medicine, the downtown department stores, politics, housing and recreation. Let's now take a look at these areas in turn as we see them today in 1972.

What impressed me with the change in the teaching profession was an experience we had in the Congress some years ago. We found that the Toronto Teachers College had engaged a rabbi to give religious instruction to the Jewish students. This, we thought, was rather incongruous because the course they were supposed to teach in the schools (which we opposed) was a course in Christianity. However, quite aside from the substantive issue the point that incidentally came to our attention was that there were ninety to one hundred Jewish students enrolled, mostly young women, with the figures rising yearly and most of them apparently—at least in those years—getting employment as elementary school teachers.

The principal of the public school nearest to where I live is a young man named Hrushevsky, of Ukrainian origin. Among the teachers on his staff are a Mr. Kurtzman, a Mrs. Feld and a Miss Goldenberg. (There are other Jewish personnel but as stated I'm only giving my casual recollections.) There are a number of principals and vice-principals scattered through Metro. I noticed there is a Jewish high school principal in Acton, Ontario. True, they're not in great numbers, but they do exist. There are numbers of Jewish department heads. There was a pattern some time ago—or so it seemed—that to reach a principalship a Jewish teacher had to have certain visible indices of assimilation—a Gentile wife for one thing, and a sort of abandonment of Jewish "markings" as it were. It would be interesting to find out if this is still true.

Two or three years ago at parents' night at the senior school my daughter attended, while visiting the teacher I saw—and the only way I could know it is by seeing—that her French teacher was Negro. Now, naturally, there's no reason why he shouldn't be Negro—which is just as it should be. However, if there had been a Negro teacher of anything when I was at school—be it manual training or grammar—just think of the sensation it would have caused! Yet my daughter had left this fact utterly unmentioned taking it as a perfectly normal fact that required no comment.

It's when we come to the universities that the radical change is noticeable. At times the campuses seem to be swarming with Jewish academic personnel be it in the social sciences, history, economics, political science, literatures (English and foreign), sciences (pure and applied) and law. The deans of the two law schools in Toronto are both Jewish, both under forty. The head of the School of Social Work at the U of T is Jewish. Looking at other cities in Canada the president of the University of Calgary (Max Wyman) and the new University of Winnipeg (Ernest Sirluck) are Jewish. An exact census of Jewish professors in the two Toronto universities hasn't been taken but the total numbers would be far more than we even suspect.

As for the engineering profession, we had a small experience in the CJC at the University a few years ago that impressed upon us the presence of engineering students. The engineering school always completes its course a month or so ahead of the other faculties. This means that its examinations often coincide with *Pesach*. In the old days it didn't matter much since so few Jewish students were enrolled and of them how many cared? But we found in the 1960s that there were a large number of Jewish undergraduates in engineering and

117

of them a sizable proportion of observant students. Eventually the head of the engineering school finally got the point and avoided the *Pesach* dates.

The implication to be drawn from the enrolment figures was, of course, that it was considered a proper profession for a Jewish boy and apparently there, too, they were being placed.

In medicine things are much different than in the mean and nasty 1920s and 1930s. Wherever one goes in hospitals whether civic or sectarian—be it Catholic or Seventh Day Adventist—one is sure to find Jewish MDs as staff doctors and department heads: at Northwestern, at General, at Humber Memorial, Scarborough, St. Joseph's, Centennial, Branson, etcetera. A few years ago a tempest blew up about a new hospital in Don Mills but even there the question was not that Jewish physicians and surgeons were not getting appointments or even senior appointments but whether certain headships were being reserved for a special in-group. Jewish medical students more and more are staying in Canada not only for their internship but for their entire careers.

What's happened with Eaton's and Simpsons? Well, there hasn't been any great influx of Jewish employees in their direction but the barriers are certainly lifted. Simpsons eliminated the barrier long before Eaton's. Recently an Eaton's ad listed the languages spoken by their employees—and at the bottom of the list was Yiddish though I'd suspect the listing, as far as use of the language was concerned, was more symbolic than real.

In politics on the local level the year 1955 was the *annus mirabilis*—the year Toronto elected a Jewish mayor and kept on re-electing him in monotonous fashion for eight years—only to elect a second one after an interval of a year.

Those few who recall the ultra-Orange complexion of Toronto's City Hall politics when membership in the Orange Order was an essential for election to the highest municipal post and appointment to the lowliest, most menial civic job can take some symbolic *nachas* out of the fact that the man Nathan Phillips defeated in December 1954 was a man who had identified Orangeism and religious bigotry with his entire political career and indeed that was the very reason he was beaten in the changed political climate that already applied in Toronto in the mid-1950s. And while we are at it, though we didn't mention the public service in our earlier summary, could we have anticipated in our earlier days that Toronto's municipal planners would be someone named Wojciech Wronski and its traffic and roads director would be a Hashomer Hatzair alumnus named Sam Cass? And aside from these senior posts a casual walk through a City Hall department would reveal many natives of Nigeria, Pakistan and states unimagined in the days of Sam McBride, Bert Wemp and Tom Foster. Would one have imagined a sign in City Hall offering them assistance in certain languages other than English? How some of our parents or grandparents would have welcomed a courtesy like that in their day! One thing might be noted: Toronto has not yet had a Catholic mayor. But it can safely be said—I hope—that it's now only because a likely candidate hasn't yet appeared.

On the national level in politics the key year was 1968, the last federal general election. In that year eight Jewish MPs were elected. The importance of this fact is not the number of Jewish MPs elected but where they were elected. It turns out that all but perhaps one were elected in ridings where the Jewish vote was negligible and certainty in no way decisive. Certainly Jack Marshall, a Newfoundland MP, has a constituency removed from the mainstream of Jewish residence. Herb Gray sits for Windsor and Max Saltsman for Galt—neither may be termed the *Yerushalayim d'Kanada*. Dave Lewis in York South (no longer attached to Forest Hill) had few Jewish electors, Phil Givens in West York even fewer and Bob Kaplan in Don Valley maybe five per cent. The only one with a traditional Jewish riding was Dave Orlikow of Winnipeg and there too he had far more non-Jews than Jews. In Toronto the Jewish ridings were represented by Ian Wahn, Mitchell Sharp and Jim Walker—all non-Jews.

What does this mean? That a Jewish political aspirant has the whole field at his disposal and is no longer confined to those areas where there is a concentration of Jewish voters. In this respect we have caught up to where Great Britain has been for many years—

119

האָרציגע באַגריסונג צו ת״ת עין חיים צום 25 יאָריגען יוביליעאָום.

ה. שאַפּסאָוויטץ און פֿאַמיליע

פֿאַרברעננט אייער זומער־וואַקאַציע אין האָטעל „מאָנטיעטה", רוססא, מאָסקאָקא
H. SHOPSOWITZ, Proprietor   295 Spadina Ave., Toronto

Jewish summer resorts flourished in an era when hotels were often "restricted."
Ad from the Toronto Hebrew Journal, 1948, for the Monteith Hotel, founded in
Muskoka in 1923 and operated by the Shopsowitz family of Toronto.

when in 1945 for instance twenty-five Jewish MPs were elected,
almost all but one or two representing non-Jewish areas.

Since I'm dealing essentially with Toronto I won't deal with
the federal civil service where there are senior appointments of
key nature such as Bernard and Sylvia Ostry, Sylva Gelber, Max
Wershoff in the diplomatic field, Simon Reisman, Louis Rasminsky,
David Gottlieb and David Golden, to name a few.

In housing, discrimination against Jewish rental or purchase in
any given area or building has almost become a thing of the past—
at least no cases have been reported or come to the community's
attention. Dr. Sidney Wax, when he was a part-time worker for
the Canadian Jewish Congress in 1948, did a survey of summer
resorts which made very clear that the words "restricted clientele"
meant "no Jews wanted." Very few complaints of this nature are
turned in these days—perhaps partly because the bias no longer
is exercised, partly because our Jewish Ontarians no longer seek
the summer hotel as much as they used to. Vacations assume other
forms and involve other places these days. The Jewish summer

120

resort of Ontario—the old Monteith Inn (or Shopsy's Shangri-La as we called it), the Gateway, Smith's Bay House, etcetera, have vanished and nothing has replaced them. However, that's beyond the orbit of this discussion. The one aspect of this kind of social bias that persists is the private social club though there, too, as in the Albany Club, a number of Jewish members now belong. The process, incidentally, was neither gradual or imperceptible. There was something of a deliberate, concerted effort before it took place.

We've traversed all the fields we touched on. Now what am I trying to say: that *Moshiyach* has arrived? That the messianic age is here? Far from it. There are still sizable pockets of resistance: the social club as mentioned, certain sections of the corporate level of the business world, Jewish clerks and stenographers still seem to be absent from the banks, the insurance companies, etcetera. Nor do we know how solid and permanent these gains are. Would a serious depression again catapult us into the same situation we knew back in the 1930s?

There are further considerations. The Fair Employment Practices Act has been on the books in this province since 1951—twenty-one years now. How much of the change is attributable to this law? How much is attributable to the improved climate of opinion? On the other hand it can be said that both the law and its existence and enforcement and the climate of opinion mutually react on and influence each other—it's a cyclical kind of development and it's hard to know where one begins and the other ends.

The question that occurs to me is: why was our community so silent in those days? Why did we endure so patiently the kind of treatment we wouldn't tolerate for a moment today?

Well, for one thing we were not the same kind of community then that we are today. We were predominantly an immigrant community, our parents were then in charge and who were they? Men and women from Russia, Poland and Roumania, not fully integrated into the society, certainly not acculturated, not yet secure in their identity and still adjusting, however imperfectly, to an unfamiliar Canadian society.

And what's more important, it was all very relative. They had come in the main from a Czarist society where Jews were regarded as an alien element, were barred from secondary (even primary) and advanced education, where to train themselves for a profession they had to cross countless hurdles including study abroad, where they were forbidden even to live in the main urban centres. In contrast to what they had been exposed to, the open society of Canada where their sons and daughters at least had a "fighting chance" at entering a college, embarking on a professional career—was so far in advance of what they knew that they were willing to put up with the discrimination obstacles which to them were challenges to be overcome.

I trust this bird's-eye view will be of assistance in appraising this segment of our community's recent history. Please bear in mind that I'm calling it a sketch—it makes no pretense at being a qualitative or even a quantitative study. Like other papers delivered in this series it's a personal document based only on subjective personal impressions. I know each one of you could multiply the cases I've mentioned and supplement episodes and incidents from other callings and professions unmentioned by me. But as stated this is a purely personal document and a more authentic study would have to be left to the social scientists. ✌

Joseph and Tania Barsh with son Preston on Spadina, ca 1940, with Goldenberg's and Shopsowitz's restaurants and Victory Theatre (formerly Standard–Strand) visible. Right, poster promoting High Holiday Services hosted by B'nai Yakov Benevolent Society with Cantor Beryl Wladofsky and Choir, Standard Theatre, ca 1930s.

Spadina Memories

THE AREA OF FIRST SETTLEMENT of Toronto's East European Jews was the Ward—the district bounded by Bay, University, Queen and Gerrard—a segment of town they shared with the Italians, then a much smaller group than today. But in the era after the First World War the Jewish community's centre of gravity shifted slightly westward to Spadina Avenue, the scene for me of countless sights, sounds and impressions from "only yesterday."

There were stormy ideological struggles within the working class of Toronto Jewry in the late 1930s when the mass of the community consisted of Yiddish-speaking immigrants. The fight within the furriers union was settled by crowbars and knuckle irons, and the Labour Lyceum on Spadina Avenue was a labour market, a political Rialto; the sidewalk in front was a hub of political discussion, as were all the restaurants and kibbetzarias up and down Spadina Avenue. Equally impressive, for that matter, was the intellectual

From the Canadian Jewish Review, November 24, 1967

123

"Toronto's Anarchist Guest," article about Emma Goldman, who resided in the city periodically in the 1920s and 1930s. Toronto Star Weekly, Dec. 31, 1926.

intensity of the political wiseacres who played chess and dominoes in obscure "stationery stores" all along the Avenue.

Spadina Avenue and its adjacent streets once hosted a thriving and vital Jewish community where Yiddish often seemed to be the *lingua franca* of the common crowd, at least among the elder generation. Who could forget *der roiter shneider*, a red-bearded tailor on Spadina to whom mothers took their unwilling boys to be fitted for a yom-tov suit of clothes? The perennial and often rowdy May Day parades of the 1930s and 1940s? The lectures by Leivik, Opatoshu, Zalman Schneiur, Melech Ravitch and others? The visits to Toronto by Sholem Asch and the whole gossipy string of eye-winking innuendo his presence would give rise to?

Yiddish stage personalities who came to town included the Adlers, Hollanders, Gehrmans, Weisenfreunds, Paul Muni, Herman Yablokoff, Morris Schwartz and Jacob ben Ami who would perform at the Standard Theatre (now the Victory Burlesque) and before that in a theatre (the Lyric) beside the Ford Hotel.

124

A Spadina Avenue landmark, Hyman's Books & Art was the locale for many literary discussions; this is the store's first location at 371 Spadina with owner Benzion Hyman in doorway. Photo taken 1925. Right, Anshei Minsk Synagogue, St. Andrew Street. (Speisman,1974)

Emma Goldman, the renowned anarchist spent her last few years in Toronto. She was considered too "dangerous" to re-enter the United States where she had lived since the age of seventeen. In 1939 I walked into the Labour Lyceum on Spadina Avenue (now a Chinese eating palace) where Goldman was billed as the speaker. I was twenty-two and knew very little about her, other than that she was seen by some as a dangerous rabble-rouser and by others as a fearless freedom fighter, but her appearance on the platform, her voice and her words, have vividly remained with me.

She spoke in Yiddish but it was a Germanized kind of Yiddish, reminiscent of the style used by public speakers and writers at the turn of the century, a style that probably came naturally to her since she had lived in the East Prussian capital of Koenigsberg as a teenager after leaving her native Kovno.

The experience is still clear in my mind. Goldman looked and talked not like the femme fatale she was rumoured to be but as a tired, aging woman, older than her seventy years. She spoke of her disappointment in the Soviet experiment which she had foreseen as far back as 1920, and her equal disillusionment in the Spanish Civil War where the opportunity for building a new society had crumbled under the guns of Franco and the brutal commissars of

Stalin. She was to die within the year. The further progress of the war and the Holocaust would only have increased her sense of loss but she was spared these further devastations.

As for local politics, who could forget the many Gentile city politicos who eagerly courted the Jewish vote, as exemplified by the various Ward Four Catholic and Protestant aldermen who started their speeches by the stock phrase "*brider und shvester*"? What a great thrill it was in 1930 when Sam Factor in Toronto West-Centre (later called Spadina) was elected over Tommy Church, who was considered unbeatable in other ridings.

The St. Andrew Synagogue—not named after the Scottish patron saint but really the Minsker Shul on that street—featured every hour-on-the-hour *minyanim* to serve the garment workers who were mourners or had *yahrzeit*. Also on Spadina, the famous Hyman's Books, where the Hebraists dropped around to discuss the latest trend in the world of literature. At the Rebbe's *hoif* on Huron Street, now the Coach House Theatre, the Galician dynasty of Stretten reigned and beer, dancing and other frivolity prevailed once a year on Simchas Torah. Concentrated in the Cecil–Beverley Street area were scores of synagogues and *shtieblekh* in the same few blocks; the area was also home to the General Zionists, Workmen's Circle, Labour Zionists, Folks Farein, Jewish Old Folks Home and other organizations.

The Pride of Israel picnics were well-attended bashes held each summer at Long Branch Park with a young, prematurely graying alderman-lawyer named Nathan Phillips as guest speaker.

Certain events and episodes are recalled with distinctly less fondness: the "Gentiles Only" placard on Brooker's Barbecue at the Humber River; the Swastika Gang at Kew Beach in 1933 and then the Pit Gang at Christie Pits and their open warfare with the Jewish boys, just as the Nazis were coming to power in Germany. ༽༼

Torah procession near the Strettener Rebbe's court on Cecil Street, ca 1940s.

A Rabbinical Dynasty on Cecil Street

THERE WERE FOUR BROTHERS as I recall them in the 1930s—Shloimele, Mord'chele, Avrumele, Isaac'le—and they were headed up by the *pere de famille* Reb Moishele, the Strettener Rebbe. The latter, the head of the dynasty, conducted his rabbinical court, his *hoif*, at a synagogue-cum-dwelling at the intersection of Cecil and Huron Streets. Mord'chele, who died much earlier than the others and whom I do not remember as clearly, had a *shtiebl* on College Street adjacent to what was then the King movie house. Avrumele at one time occupied a storefront conventicle on Clinton Street and lived on Euclid Avenue north of Bloor. Shloimele, whose beard was snow-white as far back as I recall (he seemed to look older than his father), had crossed "ethnic" lines and became spiritual advisor to the Jews of the Kiever synagogue (a Galicianer in charge of Russian Jews!)

And lastly there is Itzchok—Isaac, as Isaac'le is alternately known—the Benjamin of the sons, a totally other-worldly creature who has survived the others, a widower living alone in his house on D'Arcy Street where he communes with the *Ein Sof*, the Infinite. His wedding at his father's *hoif* in the 1930s was marred by a catastrophe—the balcony collapsed under the weight of hordes of wedding guests (and probably non-guests) resulting in broken limbs and a few concussions as wedding souvenirs.

All the brothers were known by the intimate and diminutive. It was rarely Shloime, more often Shloimele. Abraham was either

From the Canadian Jewish News, February 23, 1973.

127

Left, Reb Moishele, the Strettener Rebbe, with daughter Sarah on Cecil Street ca 1940s. Right, Rabbi Isaac'le Langner, a "totally other-worldly creature" who lived on D'Arcy Street.

Avrumele, Avremele, or even Avrumtchik. This lent an aspect of the childlike to what already was in the eye of the Jewish public an image of other-worldly ingenuousness, the simple naivete of the shtetl.

In addition to the diminutives, three of the four brothers bore special attributive tags. Abraham was also called "Der Philadelphier" because of some past connection with the city of Benjamin Franklin —a connection which was in all likelihood quite innocent but was enough to acquire the place-name. Mordecai's label was derived from closer to home, going back to the time when Toronto Junction was a separate independent community. He was called "Der Junctioner," though his stay in West Toronto might also have been quite brief.

In the 1930s, Chassidism was definitely in vogue but it was the Strettener who preserved this flame of Chassidic warmth and maintained the image of this way of life until the postwar revival, resuscitated and reinforced by the arrival of the Modzhitzer, the Bobover, the Gerer, the Lubavitcher and the other dynasties of subclans of the Chassidic hierarchies.

Some personal experiences and recollections stand out more clearly in retrospect. There were the swarms of worshippers who flocked to the West End Veteran's Hall on College Street at Crawford to *daven* with the old Rebbe (his Huron Street *bes medresh* clearly could not hold them all). There were the men and women who literally danced attendance on Avrumele on Clinton Street,

128

with a tapping of the feet and a clapping of the hand, taking hold of the inspiration he gave off. He always reminded the writer of the ample medieval friars that are seen pictured in history books and tapestries—broad of beam and jowl and enjoying life to the hilt, both on the spiritual and material levels, as God bade us.

The most rewarding experience was to spend Simchas Torah at the Rebbe's court. That evening everyone turned out: chassidim and *misnagdim*, pietist and *apikoros*, Litvak and Galicianer, believer and skeptic, to experience the joy of the Torah and, if not to give thanks for its gift, then at least to enjoy watching the "*rebbeim*" and their disciples offer up their joyous and unrestrained thanksgiving.

The procedure was most interesting. One personage in this drama, the Rebbe's *gabbai*, I believe, whose name I did not know but was known, I'm sure, to many who read this, stood out particularly. He was a tall, red-faced figure of a man, with dignity, poise and erect of posture. He cleared an immediate passageway in the crowded chaos of the shul by proclaiming in an imperious tone, in a British-inflected English, that "Gentlemen, the Rebbe is coming!" It was this British accent that I recall as something of a culture-shock. British English in this environment! Later I would say "Why not?" I was to learn of the infinite adaptability of Jews who, after all, acquired British English long before any Jews came to Canada.

Rabbi Solomon Langner's funeral obsequies befitted his station and influence. There were five eulogists—David Wohlgelernter, secretary of the synagogue; Rabbi Isaac Oelbaum who spoke of him as a colleague and friend; Rabbi Joseph Singer of New York, whose *hesped* was a melange of tears and *pilpul*; a nephew, Allan (Munish) Langner, now a Conservative rabbi in Montreal; and another nephew, Rabbi Flamm, a young Chassidic rabbi in New York.

Not an English word was spoken. It was an all-Yiddish gathering, embracing various varieties and styles of the language: Rabbi Oelbaum's Hungarian and Germanized form of the vernacular; Allan Langner's correct and bookish speech; and Flamm and Singer's idiom steeped in scripture citations, more Hebraic in vocabulary than Yiddish.

Rabbi Weds Veiled Bride Under Canopy Amid Excited Crowd

Attendees crowd the steps of the Henry Street shul to celebrate the union of two rabbinical dynasties in the wedding of Rabbi J. Twersky of New York and Pearl Langner of Toronto. From the Toronto Star, March 3, 1928.

Those in attendance were also a wide-ranging group. Not the same assembly one sees at a UJA meeting, a B'nai Brith breakfast or a Yiddish cultural lecture, though there were individuals from all of these circles. There was an investment man from the Toronto-Dominion building, a well-known surgeon, a CBC actor (son of a provincial *shoichet*), faces of working men and what used to be called *amcho*. In the gallery were women, many of them of younger age—not of the deceased's generation. The coffin was brought directly into the centre of the synagogue—an unusual measure of honour. There were no official pallbearers. Those who could shared in this mitzvah.

All had come for one purpose—to pay respect to a colorful and picturesque part of Toronto's Jewish past—a past that was quickly fading into oblivion.

Spadina & Kensington, Fact versus Fiction

FOR SOME TIME NOW it has been open season for Toronto's Spadina Avenue and its off-shoot the Kensington Market in the daily, weekly and periodical press. At one time when the *Toronto Star* and the late *Telegram* were both carrying TV and entertainment supplements, one could expect a contribution about every second or third week in either of these publications with the usual photographs of squawking ducks, a grizzly poultry *shoichet* with bloodied and feathered apron, and a montage of the Victory Burlesque, Shopsy's and the high-rise garment lofts.

Because of the interest stimulated by all this writing, bona-fide shoppers at Perlmutar's bakery have to fight their way to the counter amidst the throng of curiosity seekers and "tourists."

Magazine editors still haven't tired of assigning this story. As recent as February of this year [1972], *Toronto Life* carried a story with the same goal as all the other articles, attributing a by-now trite atmosphere of glamour, crime, double-dealing and conspiratorial intrigue to this out-sized artery that runs down Toronto's sensitive spinal column a mile west of Yonge Street.

The *Toronto Life* article suffers from an overdose of the wide-eyed naivete that seeks colour and exotic thrill at every corner and in every shop window and which goes breathless contemplating the Human Comedy that passes from Old Knox College down to Clarence Square. The older denizen of Spadina who reads it might feel akin to the character in Moliere's comedy who suddenly is told

From the Canadian Jewish News, May 12, 1972.

131

that all his life, unbeknownst to himself, he has been talking Prose!

Much is made in the familiar style of Ben Hecht and Mark Hellinger of the "pimp and the priest, artist and alcoholic" with suggestions juxtaposed of prostitution rings, razor slashings, street brawls and petty thefts.

Cornerstone of Spadina, according to the *Toronto Life* author, is the Scott Mission, purveyor of food to the down-and-outers. Surprisingly, the article fails to mention a cardinal point about its founder, the late Morris Zeidman—that this ordained Presbyterian clergyman, born in Czenstochow, was a *meshumad*—a converted Jew. (It does, however, manage to misspell his name consistently as Ziedman.) What is unintentionally amusing is how seriously and straight-faced the author reports the glamour of the haberdasher who papers his walls with signed autographs of the "show-biz" greats.

A few of the features left unmentioned that escaped her attention: that the Standard Theatre, now the Victory Burlesque, is the only building in North America—perhaps the world—that was constructed for the purpose of housing a Yiddish theatre; that the Crescent Grill has as many Damon Runyon types as the drugstore at Dundas and Spadina—and the same applies, with the addition of the occasional Talmud *chochem*, to Ladowsky's United Bakers; that the Homestead restaurant in its day was a real centre of the bohemian-intellectual elite; that the noted anarchist Emma Goldman used to lecture at the Labour Lyceum and other Spadina Avenue halls (to say nothing of Melech Ravitch, Zalman Schneiur and the entire galaxy of Jewish political and poetic figures).

Moreover, this list could be expanded indefinitely for the irony is that there is history and colour inscribed in every brick on the Avenue but not in the lurid tones and categories that *Toronto Life* paints.

Some day an article will be written on Spadina that will truly tell its story. In the meantime, editors will continue to assign the kind of article that paints the melodrama thick, heavy—and phony. In the meantime, editors, please—don't overwork the theme in such an underdone way. ∽

A Toronto Prizefighter Tells His Story

SAM LUFTSPRING'S AUTOBIOGRAPHY *Call Me Sammy* (published 1975) is about growing up in the College and Spadina section of Toronto, a story of the demi-monde of boxers, racetrack characters, taxicab drivers, of bootlegging as it was carried on in Nassau Street and other Kensington area offshoots in the 1920s and the hungry 1930s, of the open gaming houses of Will Morrissey and Abe Orpen. It's a story built around Toronto by a man closely bound up and identified with the city and very much in love with it. It takes one back to the old Ontario before the days of civil rights and anti-discrimination, when the sports columnists and reporters of the big city dailies (yes, even the liberal *Daily Star*) wrote about the "aggressive little Jew-boy"; when the scribes called any Jewish pugilist a "Hebe fighter" or a "son of Moses" and no one took offense (or seemed to).

It's a story about what happens when a promising young fighter

From The Canadian Jewish News, November 21, 1975.

North side of College Street between Borden and Brunswick, 1958.

has won the Canadian title, is in sight of the world championship and suddenly through a freak accident—which is really not such a freak after all, considering the intensive pummeling boxers are subject to—he loses the sight of an eye, his entire world collapses, and his greatest fear is that he will wind up a bum—a real fear considering what happened to many of his contemporaries. It's also a story of a Jewish father determined to publicly assert and demonstrate this "non-bum" status even if it means following economist Thorsten Veblen's theories of conspicuous consumption and financing his son's $5,000 bar mitzvah through sale of a taxicab.

It's likewise a story that touches on the organized Jewish community. How many of us knew that when Luftspring and Baby Yack took their abortive sea voyage to participate in the anti-Fascist Olympics in Barcelona in 1936, they were staked by a fund-raising stag sponsored by the Canadian Jewish Congress presided over by the staid son of England, the late O. B. Roger? And who among us recalls that on July 7, 1936, a letter from Luftspring and Yack appeared in the Toronto *Globe* in which the two young men proudly and with dignity renounced any intention of participating in the Olympic Games of Nazi Berlin. "The German government," they wrote, "is treating our brothers and sisters like dogs."

Luftspring's book makes no secret that the writing is "as told to" Brian Swarbrick. No one would suspect the Elizabeth Street-born

134

fighter of harbouring literary talent. But the ghostwriter does an excellent job of giving it Luftspring's articulation.

Unlike most of his contemporaries, Luftspring did not come to boxing through street fighting or brawling. He was, he tells us, the babied younger son in a family of protective older sisters from whom he never heard a harsh word. It was the smokers on Queen Street West held above the old Mary Pickford Cinema and the lure of fame and attention that gave him incentive and motivation for the fight game and made him polish, study and sharpen his reflexes. Throughout the book he waxes nostalgic and sentimental about College and Spadina, attributing values and experiences that helped mould him and acknowledging his eternal debt—doing his bit to create a mythology designed to outdo Mordecai Richler's rival St. Urbain Street in Montreal.

The Jewish component is a strong thread throughout the book. His father's relationship to the Slipier *shtiebl*, his New York manager Al Weill's burning desire to create a Jewish world champ, his brushes with anti-Semites, his renunciation of the Berlin Olympics—one thing is quite certain: Luftspring has never suffered from an identity crisis. To paraphrase his older literary contemporary whom he failed to meet when he stopped in Paris en route to Barcelona: "A Jew is a Jew is a Jew."

There is one episode involving the Jewish community in which he probably participated that this writer regrets he didn't mention. It was the famous "Social and Athletic Division" of the first United Jewish Appeal in Toronto in that big first year of 1948 when the prize fighters, hotel habitués, ex-bootleggers and bookmakers organized their stint for the newly-formed Jewish state and the participants were the Damon Runyon personages he mentions with names like Mexican Pete, Joe the Goof, Maxie Chicago, Pork Chops, Freddy the Beast and other colourful tags which sound lifted right out of *Guys and Dolls* but which this reviewer can vouch were real.

Call Me Sammy isn't a great book, nor a startling book, but it's a good book, warm and nostalgic, and it will bring back a pleasant taste and flavour of an era only just departed. ❧

Lady Eaton and John David Eaton, possibly
at opening of College Street store, 1930.

Eaton's and the Jews

THE DECLINE AND FALL of the Eaton's merchandising empire
and of the Eaton dynasty has produced a mixture of feelings:
sentiment, nostalgia, even some mild annoyance. It has also inspired
some thoughts under the category of "Eaton's and the Jews."

The Eaton policy of banning the hiring of Jewish employees—
except in the tailoring shops where they were indispensible—was
well known. It should be borne in mind, of course, that this was
not peculiar to Eaton's. It was a practice prevalent in the retail and
office administration fields. With Eaton's, however, it seemed to
last longer and reached right into the 1940s and 1950s. Cases can be
cited by many of those now entering their seventies. But there was
never any sign of counter-boycott by the Jewish housewife. Far from
it. In the early days of Jewish settlement a century ago, the Toronto
flagship store and its factories were located only steps away from the
Ward and the *balebatim* had only to walk a few minutes from their
homes on Teraulay or Chestnut Street to capture the *metziyes* that
were offered.

But that is not the whole story. To complete the picture, one story
of interfaith beneficence may be told, though it does not appear in
Rod McQueen's recent book on Eaton's. It involved a young Jewish
tailor from the Polish shtetl of Ostrovtze named Yossel Shlisky, and

From Fraternally Yours, July-August 1999

Lady Eaton, spouse of Sir John Eaton. She was a woman who took a personal, maternal interest in the welfare of the families of workers. According to Stephen Speisman, Ontario's Jewish archivist, Lady Eaton was making a tour of operations in the factories when she heard someone singing at work. Impressed by the quality of his voice, she learned he was a Jewish immigrant from Poland and had musical ambitions which he had to forsake to make a living.

Lady Eaton must have been impressed, for she signed him up at the Royal Conservatory from which he graduated with honors. He went on to become a recognized *chazzan* throughout North America and Europe. His records, according to the late Nathan Stolnitz in *The Wings of Song*, were circulated all over the Jewish world.

Where was this story kept and preserved? Among families and compatriots from Ostrovtze. Dr. Speisman's grandparents stem from that town. ❧

Pieces by Stephen A. Speisman

Born in Toronto in 1943, Stephen Speisman grew up near Bathurst Street and Dovercourt Road before moving to North York as a young teenager. He studied American history as an undergraduate at the University of Toronto, but changed his focus for his graduate studies. His doctoral thesis served as the basis for his book, *The Jews of Toronto: A History to 1937,* which was published by McClelland and Stewart in 1979. Still widely regarded as the the most important work on the subject, the book won a City of Toronto Book Award in 1980 and has since appeared in multiple editions. Dr. Speisman was the founding director of the Ontario Jewish Archives and served as its director from 1973 to 1999. In 2001 he became executive director of the Toronto Hebrew Memorial Park (Pardes Shalom Cemetery). He wrote numerous essays and articles about the Jews of Toronto for the *Canadian Jewish News*, the *Dictionary of Canadian Biography* and other publications. "He had an unparalleled knowledge of Toronto's Jewish history," the *Canadian Jewish News* said upon his death in 2008.

Building at 111 Elizabeth Street at Cuttle Place, south of Dundas, ca 1974 (Speisman) and below in 1937. Building at extreme left housed a Yiddish printing shop.

140

Same buildings are visible in this view of Elizabeth Street south from Dundas, 1966, showing City Hall and Lichee Gardens on right.

St. John's Shtetl: the Ward in 1911

ST. JOHN'S WARD, a district bounded roughly by Yonge Street, University Avenue, Queen and College streets, was one of the first speculative developments on park lots in Toronto. Originally called "Macaulay-town," it was already subdivided by the middle of the nineteenth century, most of the buildings standing sixty years later being one- or two-storey stuccoed frame cottages dating from the 1850s and 1860s. Typical of developments of this sort, many of the streets were short and close together, punctuated by alleys and laneways bearing names such as Cuttle Place, Foster Place and Price's Lane.

"The Ward," as it was popularly known, was considered a slum from the beginning, its status confirmed by the placing of the local

From Gathering Place: Peoples and Neighbourhoods of Toronto, 1834–1945. Robert F. Harney, Ed. Multicultural History Society of Ontario, 1985.

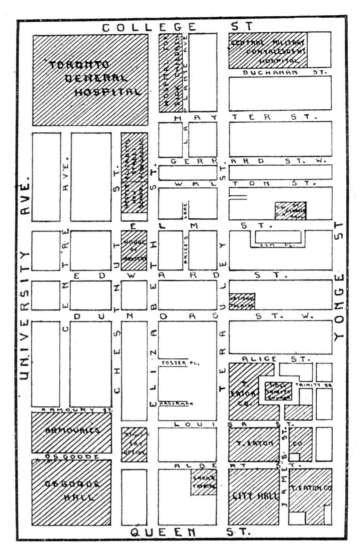

Map from 1918 booklet, "What is 'the Ward' going to do with Toronto?" Bureau of Municipal Affairs, Toronto.

poor house—the House of Industry—at Elm and Chestnut streets in 1848. Centre Street (later Centre Avenue) was considered a red-light district until late in the century.[1] The population of the area was largely English-speaking, but the Ward was destined to become a major immigrant reception area by the turn of the century, and the principal component of its population would be East European Jews.

The earliest Jewish residents in Toronto—English, Germans and those from Quebec—had settled farther east along King Street, in the commercial centre of mid-nineteenth-century Toronto, and when they grew prosperous enough to live separately from their places of business, they continued to be found east of Yonge Street. These individuals never lived in a bloc; they did not succeed in creating, nor did they seek to build, a Jewish enclave within the larger community. The last two decades of the century, however, saw a transformation in the Jewish population of Toronto, indeed of all North America, as large-scale emigration from Eastern Europe resulted in an influx of thousands escaping the persecution and economic difficulties of their homelands. Until immigration was curtailed temporarily by the outbreak of the First World War, the Jewish population of Toronto grew dramatically, from a little over 3,000 in 1901 to about 9,000 in 1907. By 1911 there were over 18,000 Jews in the city.[2] Almost without exception, those who arrived from Eastern Europe in this period gravitated to St. John's Ward. First to appear were the Lithuanians and Galicians, whose livelihoods had been threatened by the advent of the industrial revolution. Then came Jews from Russia and Russian Poland, seeking to avoid the restrictions of the May Laws and the hazards of the pogrom. The latter, impoverished by comparison to many of the Litvakim and Galicianer who were able to bring some financial resources with them, soon constituted a majority of the Jews living in the city.[3]

The earliest East Europeans came as individuals, hoping eventually to bring their families, or themselves to return to Europe. By the end of the century, however, emigration of entire families was the rule. They came in search of the *goldene medinah*, the golden land, and that certainly was not Toronto. Some settled here because they had run out of money on the way to some locality in the United States, perhaps Chicago. Nevertheless, once there was a nucleus of Jews here, urging their relatives and *landsleit* to come, often sending back photographs of well-dressed Toronto Jews which bore little resemblance to reality, emigrants began to set out bound specifically for Toronto. Certainly by 1900, this was the case.[4] Most of those who arrived prior to the turn of the century settled to the south of what would become the core of St. John's Ward, along Richmond

Elevated view of Eaton's factories and warehouses, ca 1910. Yonge and Queen intersection is at extreme left (off), City Hall behind smokestack, Holy Trinity Church at lower right.

Street between Yonge and York and on York Street itself. Some of the more substantial families (relatively speaking) did, however, settle north of Queen Street; the Lithuanian synagogue, the first permanent East European congregation in the city [Goel Tzedec], opened at University Avenue and Elm Street in 1883.

By the late 1890s, however, increasing numbers of Jews were moving north and west of the intersection of Queen and Yonge, until by 1900 Jews outnumbered all others in the Ward, the first time they were to do so in any district in the city. Over the next decade they would create, in these few square blocks, a miniature Jewish civilization in the heart of Anglo-Saxon Toronto, reaching its peak in the half-dozen years prior to the First World War. They did not set out to create a ghetto, but many soon discovered the advantage of reconstructing, as far as was possible, the amenities and the security of the *shtetl*.

Jews settled in the Ward initially because they had little choice; they needed inexpensive accommodation close to steady employment immediately upon their arrival. The European experience had taught them the value of living adjacent to the commercial centre of the city, and in St. John's Ward the right conditions obtained. Few had skills that could be used in North America. Restrictions upon Jews in Eastern Europe had limited the crafts into which they were admitted. Most had some mercantile experience, but even the most petty enterprise demanded some small amount of capital.

144

Even peddling required at least credit. The alternative was to find employment in the factory.

It was in the field of ready-made clothing that the Jews found employment here as in other North American cities. The reasons for this phenomenon have been detailed sufficiently elsewhere and need not be elaborated here.[5] Suffice it to say that the Ward was in convenient proximity to this industry. In the early years of the twentieth century, the major clothing firms, the Lowndes Company, Johnson Brothers and others were located on Front Street, Wellington Street, Church and Bay. By 1910 the T. Eaton Company, which would become the largest single employer of Jews from St. John's Ward, had established an enormous manufacturing complex in the streets bounded by Teraulay (now Bay), Albert, Louisa and James.

Factory operatives preferred to live close to their places of employment. They worked long hours and wanted to minimize travelling time; they sought to avoid spending money on streetcars by walking to work; they needed a variety of employment opportunities, for although day-hiring was rare, the introduction of the piecework system reduced the skill required for specific tasks and so heightened competition for jobs. Seasonal layoffs and strikes made employment even more precarious. St. John's Ward, therefore, developed as an immigrant reception area adjacent to the central business district, in much the same way as similar areas appeared throughout the continent. While all Jews certainly did not work in the factories, it was their presence, combined with the availability of relatively inexpensive housing, that drew Jewish immigrants to the Ward.[6]

Working conditions in Toronto factories nowhere approximated the appalling situation that existed in the Lower East Side of New York or even in Montreal. Indeed, by the standards of the time the atmosphere at Eaton's, for instance, was very good. Orthodox Jews could take Saturday mornings off without fear of dismissal and one could earn a little extra by informally instructing boys sent by their parents to learn the trade. And in general, because rents were not

Six families lived in this rear-lane tenement near City Hall (14 Teraulay) and there was a factory on the third floor. Sole source of water was an outdoor tap; the privy at right served 40 persons. Winter, 1912.

excessively high in the Ward prior to the First World War, few had to engage in homework.[7] Nevertheless, a significant number of Jews avoided the factory if they could, and for a variety of reasons. Some simply were uncomfortable working for non-Jews;[8] the major firms were still not in Jewish hands. Others would not work on Saturday mornings, when a majority of the establishments remained open and would make no provision for Sabbath observance. Still others could not abide the restriction of set working hours, preferring to continue the European tradition of morning and evening synagogue attendance and religious study.

If the solution was to strike out on their own, their choices were limited. They had virtually no capital and in many enterprises they had not the traditional skills to compete with non-Jewish immigrants. Consequently, independent Jewish "businessmen" were generally to be found in the salvage trades, as rag-pickers, bottle collectors, used furniture dealers or as peddlers. Peddling and the salvage trades were low on the scale of occupational prestige—a factor which lessened competition from other groups—but they had the advantage of allowing the Jew to maintain his independence and, indeed, his dignity within the Jewish community. Status, prior to the First World War, still depended largely upon piety and learning rather than upon wealth.[9] By 1916, Jewish rag-pickers alone would number 600 in Toronto.[10]

The ultimate in independence, of course, was the occupant of the retail or artisan's shop: the barber, shoemaker, grocer, restaurateur, pawnbroker, second-hand or drygoods dealer. Such enterprises abounded in the Ward, serving the local population, but so many businesses of similar type were compressed into so small an area that competition was fierce and often the storekeeper could neither support his family on this endeavour alone nor employ his own grown children. Members of the family, therefore, engaged in a variety of occupations, some tending the store, others engaging in peddling or working in the factories. Others still did contract work in their homes for the large needle-trade firms.

Living conditions in St. John's Ward in the first decade of the twentieth century were not nearly as bad as those in immigrant districts in other large cities in the United States,[11] but by Toronto standards they were deplorable. In 1911 there were eighty-two people per acre, a higher density than in any other part of Toronto except the predominantly Anglo-Celtic Cabbagetown;[12] and in view of the smaller buildings in St. John's Ward, the density per room, if not per acre, could be as high as elsewhere. On the average, there were six to eight people per building—the overwhelming majority of these, it will be recalled, were cottages—but some housed as many as ten to fifteen. Most structures had three to five rooms, with the amount of living space being diminished by the presence of the workshops and sewing machines of home industry. Few barracks-like tenements appeared in the Ward; in 1911, there were only eight such structures, as well as several hotels converted into boarding houses. Jews appear to have avoided these, primarily because their rents were exorbitant. The municipal authorities imposed no limit on the number of people who could inhabit a given structure and

View of Wineberg Apartments, Teraulay Street, 1910, a building that was designed to alleviate slumlike conditions in the Ward. Architectural drawing with original caption, from the journal Construction, 1907, appears opposite.

consequently large families crowded into the cottages, together with *landsleit* from Europe and boarders taken in to supplement the family income. Most of these cottages in the early years of the century appear to have been rented from non-Jews.

While the moral tone of the Ward improved as the population became predominantly Jewish, physical conditions deteriorated rapidly. The occasional prosperous Jewish investor attempted to improve conditions in the area by erecting modern brick row houses on Chestnut and Armoury streets about 1908–1909;[13] these efforts were too few to make much difference. Large numbers of Jews arrived from Europe and settled in the Ward between 1905 and 1912; the demand for housing increased, rents soared and landlords, hoping to make a substantial profit as the commercial and administrative sector of the city expanded westward, neglected to improve their properties. Dr. Charles Hastings, the Medical Health Officer, reported in 1911 that 108 houses in the Ward were unfit for habitation, yet most were occupied. Some barely kept out the elements. One structure housed three families in five rooms, one of which contained two sewing machines as well. Another cottage, rented for an astronomical $20 a month, had four feet of water in its basement. Almost a third of the structures had no plumbing or drainage; waste was simply thrown into the yards.[14] Conditions in the rear cottages—that is, those built in the laneways behind cottages fronting the streets, by landlords

148

Front Elevation, Wineberg Apartments, in the "Ward," Toronto. A noteworthy design of moderate priced
apartments. A style of building most needed in the congested districts of our larger cities. A good
example of a plain, simple, economical structure in which the designer has accomplished
his purpose without the useless expenditure of money on unnecessary ornamentation.
Fred Herbert, Architect.

attempting to maximize the profits from their properties—were the
worst. Surrounded by stables, privies and yards full of garbage, the
occupants found the odour so foul that they hesitated to open their
windows even in summer.

By 1911 congestion had reached alarming proportions and
was aggravated by the encroachment of the Eaton complex and
the municipal buildings on the residential portion of the area.
In that year, a large block of land at College and Elizabeth
streets was expropriated and cleared as a site for the new Toronto
General Hospital and, to make matters worse, the city would soon
expropriate the area bounded by Louisa, Albert, Elizabeth and
Chestnut to make way for a new Registry Office.[15] Rear tenements
demonstrated the worst conditions, each divided into dwellings of
six dark and tiny rooms. Yet these commanded exorbitant rents; in
some cases families living in one room had to take in boarders to
help pay for them. One three-storey structure on Teraulay Street,
specifically mentioned in Hastings' report, had a factory on the top
floor, while the outhouse adjacent to the building was shared by
thirty residents and the forty employees of the factory. In winter it
was generally frozen. Behind the row was a privy which had been
overflowing for some time, but was rented to the occupants of a
front house for the outrageous sum of $10 a month. Jews tended to
avoid such accommodation; but at the time the report was compiled,

149

Cartoon at left, ca 1914, shows Medical Health Officer Dr. Charles Hastings scrubbing 'Toronto's Slum Element' and exclaiming, 'I had no idea you needed cleaning up so badly'. Cartoon at right, ca 1914, shows Dr. Hastings taking large container of disinfectant into Toronto's 'Foreign Colony' where 'overcrowded' and 'unhealthy unsanitary conditions' prevail.

some Jews were living in this particular tenement, although they were gone within several months.[16] It should be noted that none of these tenement rows or converted hotels was owned by Jews.

Jewish householders in the Ward, as the assessment rolls indicate, tended to be young as compared to non-Jewish residents. In the case of the latter, women were widows and men were over fifty. This suggests that many were long-time residents, having arrived before the advent of the Jews. The relative youthfulness of the Jewish householder, however, does not mean that there were few elderly Jewish residents; immigrant ghettos, in general, do exhibit a higher proportion of young to old than do districts inhabited by the native-born. Jewish families tended to emigrate when the father was in his twenties or early thirties; the elderly often refused to leave Europe until they were persuaded to come at a later time or until the family was financially capable of supporting them. Once here, they lived with their children and consequently do not often appear on the assessment rolls. The youthfulness of the population was reflected also in the large number of children under the age of fourteen. Even married children continued to live under their parents' roof, the extended family being typical of the immigrant ghetto throughout North America.

By 1911 the Ward, together with the few blocks between

150

University Avenue and McCaul Street, had become virtually a self-contained community as regards Jewish services and cultural, religious and educational facilities. A rich variety of service and retail shops, run by Jews and generally catering exclusively to them, operated throughout the area. Some, like Dworkin's News Agency on Elizabeth Street, the offices of the various Jewish steamship agents, or the multitude of kosher restaurants, became important social and political centres for the area. At Dworkin's, for instance, one could read copies of the Yiddish press imported from New York, and discuss the latest philosophies of social change or the efforts of labour unions throughout the continent. Once the local Yiddish-language paper, the *Yidisher Zhurnal*, began to publish in 1912, Dworkin's became its major distribution centre. Of less cosmic significance, but nevertheless important, were institutions such as Halpern's seltzer factory, which perpetuated the comforts of the *shtetl* on Chestnut Street. The seasoned observer could always spot the establishments which claimed superiority, be it in the field of food, laundry or plumbing; they were invariably signified by the designation "New York."

After 1909, a Jewish day nursery and a free dispensary were available on Elizabeth Street south of Agnes (Dundas). The former enabled mothers who had to work outside the home to do so with relative peace of mind. The dispensary was a direct attempt to counter missionary activities, especially those of the Presbyterians, who provided such facilities in order to attract parents and children into the missions. Presided over by Dora Goldstick, a young Toronto midwife trained in Ohio, and Abe Hashmall, the first Jewish graduate in pharmacy at the University of Toronto, the dispensary would eventually grow into Mount Sinai Hospital.

Formal entertainment was to be had in the institution of the Yiddish theatre, at first at the National in the former Lithuanian synagogue on University Avenue, and later at the Lyric which, after 1909, occupied a former Methodist church at the northeast corner of Agnes and Teraulay (Dundas and Bay). Local companies and those from New York and Detroit were popular attractions whose

'This is a daily scene at the Hospital for Sick Children where many Jewish babies are taken care of among those of other nationalities.' Canadian Jewish Review, December 29, 1922.

repertoire ranged from riotous and occasionally risque comedy to Shakespeare and tragedies of heartrending capacities. The latter served a dual purpose; in the absence of a psychiatric service, the tragedy provided the struggling immigrant, especially the overburdened housewife, an inexpensive opportunity for catharsis. However much *tzores* one had, the character on the stage had infinitely more, and for a few pennies, one could go to the theatre and have a good cry. Productions too large for the Lyric could be staged at Massey Hall, within easy walking distance of the Ward.

The most ubiquitous institution in the Ward, however, was the synagogue. By 1911 a majority of Toronto congregations were still located in the Ward where they had been founded. A few, such as Goel Tzedec on University Avenue (the Lithuanian synagogue, opened 1907) and Machzikei HaDas on Teraulay Street (a Galician synagogue established in 1906) were housed in spacious structures built for the purpose; indeed, Goel Tzedec, the largest such building in the city with a capacity of 1,200, was modeled on the Roman

Goel Tzedec on University Avenue was the largest synagogue in the city. Constructed 1906, consecrated February 1907, demolished 1955 after the congregation joined with 'McCaul' to found Beth Tzedec.

Catholic Cathedral of Westminster. Other congregations occupied converted churches (e.g., Shomrei Shabbos, Chestnut Street) or remodeled stores or cottages. Each ethnic grouping or group of townsmen as a rule insisted upon its own synagogue, where the peculiar customs of its European locality could be meticulously observed. So numerous had they become that Centre Avenue, only a few blocks long, had four major congregations on it in 1911 and probably also several *shtieblekh* (cottage synagogues) which do not appear in the municipal records. The synagogue was the anchor for the majority of Jews living in St. John's Ward, providing a social and cultural centre as well as a place to pray. Facilities for charity organizations and social gatherings were provided, as well as opportunities for religious education for adults and children alike. The latter were still informal in 1911. Efforts to establish congregational schools in the East European synagogues would not come to fruition until 1914.[17]

Formal Jewish education for children in the Ward was still, in 1911, provided on four levels: by the incompetent *"siddur melamed,"*

Louis Singer was the city's second Jewish alderman and the first elected after 1900; a sparkling orator, he eventually entered the legal profession. Photo from Yiddish newspaper, ca 1914. Right, Conservative Party headquarters in the Ward, with Yiddish sign, 1911. From The Jews in Canada, a Christian missionary booklet.

usually someone inept at business, who hawked whatever little knowledge he had door-to-door; by the capable private teacher who either set up a *cheder*, a one-room school, in part of his own home or taught in the homes of individual pupils; by the congregational school at Holy Blossom on Bond Street; or by the community schools. Of the last, there were two in 1911, one religious and one secularist; both were located on Simcoe Street, on the western periphery of the Ward.

The Toronto Hebrew Religion School, or Simcoe Street Talmud Torah as it was usually known, had been established in 1907 through the efforts of Rabbi Jacob Gordon, the spiritual leader of the Lithuanian and Russian communities, together with the lay leaders of both of his congregations, University Avenue and McCaul Street. Its purpose was to provide education on a high level, in contrast to the abominably low standards tolerated by the employers of most of the private teachers and the bare minimum of traditional subjects taught at Holy Blossom. The intention was to attract the children of all Jews regardless of ethnic origin or religious position, but by 1911 it had come to be viewed essentially as the Lithuanian Talmud Torah. The Polish Jews and many of the Galicians were alienated by its modernist approach: its approval of secular subjects (although none were yet taught), its Zionist leanings, and the fact that the language of instruction was Hebrew rather than Yiddish. The dissidents, under the leadership of Rabbi Joseph Weinreb, the rabbi of the Galician community, and Rabbi Yudal Rosenberg of

154

the Polish community, who would arrive in 1912, did not yet have the resources to set up a school of their own. It was not far off, but in the interim, private tutoring continued to be the rule.

The extreme orthodox were not alone in their opposition to Simcoe Street. Toronto now had a sizeable minority of secularist Jews, many having escaped after the abortive Russian revolution of 1905. These wanted a Jewish education to promote the idea of peoplehood, without the religious trappings which they considered irrelevant to their lives. Their ideologies were varied: socialist, territorialist, anarchist, communist. But they had a common bond, a sympathy for the working class, and a belief in the necessity of perpetuating Jewish culture through the Yiddish language and of bridging the gap between immigrant parents and their children. To this end they founded the Jewish National Radical School in September 1911, under the leadership of dedicated individuals such as Isaac Matenko, who held down a factory job during the day and taught in the evenings.

A final Jewish institution in the Ward deserves mention: the mutual benefit society. In a system in which public welfare was virtually unthinkable, both on the part of the government and on the part of the potential recipient, a mechanism had to be found to help the immigrant over the difficult times following his arrival and to assist him in bringing other members of his family from the old country. For many, the synagogue provided these services: moral support, interest-free loans, credit to purchase merchandise or a wagon, contacts to employment. For others, however, secular organizations were preferred, some cutting across ethnic lines (e. g., the Toronto Hebrew Benevolent Society, founded 1899, and the Pride of Israel Sick Benefit Society, founded 1905). Still others organized *landsmanshaften*, composed of individuals from the same locality in Europe. Too numerous to mention individually, these organizations provided emotional and often economic stability to the Jews of St. John's Ward. They were perhaps the strongest link between life in Toronto and the *shtetl* of Eastern Europe.

By 1911, therefore, Jewish society in St. John's Ward was virtually self-contained. One ventured forth to work for non-Jews in the factories, to gather junk in the city or to peddle in the hinterland, but for most it was only out of necessity. Few residents of the Ward dared yet consider themselves a part of the larger Toronto society. Fewer still would have ventured to support a Jew for municipal office, let alone stand oneself for election. Those who did so in the first decade of the century were not taken seriously.[18] Granted, there were political concerns. One would like to feel he had a friend at City Hall when peddling licences were necessary, when gas rates had to be guaranteed or when one ran afoul of the law by stabling a horse illegally. But the consensus was that a Jew would be isolated at council and that the most advantageous course lay in cultivating the Orange establishment.

In 1911 Toronto Jews still had no Yiddish newspaper that would serve, as the *Forward* was doing in New York, to urge participation on the political scene. Nevertheless, over the previous decade, political awareness had been growing in the Ward, for the mundane issues just mentioned, but also out of a genuine desire to understand and participate in the Canadian political process as befits the citizens of a democratic society. Indeed, the residents of the Ward demonstrated surprising enthusiasm and interest in the federal election that year. As one observer remarked, "every man, woman and child in the ward was a politician . . . ."[19] Under these circumstances, the potential for corruption was great, as ward heelers were not above purchasing the votes their candidates required with favours and dollars. Some of the more acculturated and politically astute Jews, therefore, had established the Hebrew Ratepayers Association in 1909, not only to lobby for Jewish interests, but also to channel this growing political awareness, through education, to "a higher standard of citizenship."

While the Hebrew Ratepayers professed to be non-partisan, urging support of the best candidate regardless of affiliation, there existed in the Ward, as early as 1910, a Hebrew Conservative Association, which was considered a force worthy of attention by local members of Parliament. By 1911 the residents of the Ward were beginning to have enough confidence to support Jewish candidates,

Photographer William James's superb elevated view of Agnes and Teraulay (Dundas and Bay) from an Eaton's building, 1910, looking northwest towards the Ontario Legislature, with the Teraulay Street Synagogue (Machzikei Hadas, built 1907) in foreground and the Lyric Yiddish Theatre in a former church at centre right.

these being especially numerous—although unsuccessful—in the municipal elections of 1913. Eventually, in 1914, Louis Singer, a scion of the East European community, albeit now a member of Holy Blossom, would be elected alderman in Ward Four, representing the area west of University Avenue.

Social status and social mobility operated in the Ward on two levels: community leadership, either religious or secular, and in the area of economics. Rabbis Weinreb and Gordon, representing the Galician and Lithuanian communities respectively, still exerted considerable influence among their followers; members of the Goldstick family took the lead, for instance, among secularist

157

'Foreigners swearing to their true identify and qualifications' at voters' registration booth in the Ward. Toronto Star, March 1908.

intellectuals; the major Jewish employers—Mendel Granatstein, for example, who operated a waste-processing concern at Agnes and University—unpopular as they may have been, were nonetheless considered to have made it. Most residents of the Ward, however, were not concerned with their status in the total Jewish community; they concentrated on improving themselves economically and on providing the best possible living conditions for their families.

The assessment rolls indicate that by 1911, an increasing number of Jewish residents of the Ward, indeed of Ward residents generally, were owners of their properties. About half of the buildings in the area by this time were owned by residents of the Ward and half of these by their occupants. Jewish owners were not necessarily self-employed craftsmen or storekeepers as one would expect; "operators" appear frequently among the lists of property owners and peddlers, too, were not absent, although a majority of these did continue to rent. There seems to have been some correspondence between length of residence in the city and ownership, but it is not improbable that some of the prosperous preferred to invest their money elsewhere in expectation of greater profit or were saving to bring relatives from Europe.

158

'M. Milgram, Barber Shop' reads the window sign. Toronto, perhaps ca 1910–1914.

There is evidence of hierarchies among members of particular occupations; a peddler could make his living with anything from a backpack to a handcart or a horse-drawn conveyance. The nature of the goods he sold often determined his status as much as his means of transporting them. And some peddlers, through good business sense or the luck of having on hand goods in demand, did exceedingly well.

By 1911 one can discern the presence of Jewish owners of Ward property living outside the area, usually between University Avenue and Bathurst Street, south of Bloor. But almost invariably, they had lived in the Ward during the previous decade. For Jews in the Ward, removal west of University Avenue was indicative of achievement. In some cases, the move was accompanied by changes in occupation, demonstrating upward mobility. For instance, Israel Greisman was a peddler living on Chestnut Street in 1905, whereas in 1911 he was a rentier living on what is now Dundas Street near McCaul. Another peddler, Simon Rabinovitch, also living on Chestnut Street in 1905, had moved to Beverley Street by 1911 and was listed as having been engaged in real estate. Nevertheless, for those living outside the Ward, upward movement had not been

Two-storey commercial-residential buildings on Elizabeth Street, ca 1913 in the heart of the Jewish ghetto; several of the signs on the walls are in Yiddish.

rapid; most had been living in Toronto prior to 1895. Only shortly before 1911 did relatively large-scale movement out of the Ward begin to take place.

It is difficult, on the basis of such a limited study, to say much with accuracy about the speed of upward mobility of those Jews remaining in the Ward in 1911. Since the actual census documents are still [1977] closed to researchers, it is impossible to determine, for example, when each resident arrived in Canada. Although the assessment rolls indicate that virtually every Jewish householder held the municipal franchise in 1911, this required only three years residence under the act of 1906. One can say something, however, about physical mobility. The rapidity with which occupants of particular dwellings changed is striking; there was often a complete turnover in the few months between the compilation of the city directory and that of the assessment rolls. Indeed, there was probably even greater movement than the assessment rolls suggest, since they do not take into account the non-taxpaying lodger.

In total, one can discover three types of movement among Jews

These rundown buildings on Elizabeth Street ca 1937 are the same as those that appear opposite. Note the clock tower of City Hall in the background. After a decades-long tug of war, the once-Jewish street became the heart of Chinatown.

of the Ward in this period. One group moved several times within the Ward, a sign of economic difficulty. It was not unusual for such people to leave the city within five years. A second category consisted of those who moved out of the Ward but to areas of the same character, for instance to the slums of Niagara Street, near the municipal abattoir. All movement out of the Ward, therefore, did not demonstrate improved social and economic status. Finally, there were those who moved westward toward Spadina Avenue in the half-dozen years following 1911. These constituted a majority, the upwardly mobile who followed the prosperous Jewish professionals and entrepreneurs who had moved west of University Avenue prior to 1911. As was the case with the latter, the move was often accompanied by a change in occupation; grocers became real estate agents, tailors clothing manufacturers and carpenters contractors. Most appear to have retained their occupations but to have achieved a measure of success in them. For this last group, especially, a minimum period of eight to ten years in Toronto seems to have been a prerequisite for such a move. As a rule, elderly shopkeepers remained in the Ward while their children moved westward. A similar pattern is evident among elderly non-Jews as well, but it would appear that Jews over the age of fifty were more mobile than non-Jews in the same age group.[20]

By 1911, the Ward had achieved the apex of its development

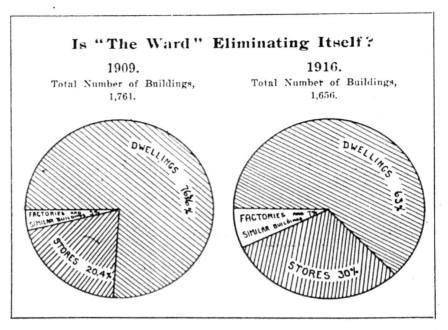

Chart showing decrease in number of residences and increase in number of factories and stores in the Ward from 1909 to 1916. From 'What is the Ward Going to Do with Toronto?', 1918.

as a Jewish area and had generated enough inertia to maintain itself as a self-contained community, even as many of its residents were economically capable of leaving it. The presence of Jewish institutions, retail shops and other amenities, coupled with the secure Yiddish-speaking atmosphere, was a powerful cohesive. Nevertheless, the seeds of the Ward's disintegration as a Jewish district had been sown as early as 1904, when a catastrophic fire destroyed a major segment of Toronto's manufacturing district. Many of the ready-made clothing factories which employed residents of the Ward had been located in the heart of the area devastated by the fire. When these firms resumed production, they chose new quarters to the west, often along Wellington, Richmond and Adelaide streets between York Street and Spadina Avenue. The pattern of disruption for Jewish factory workers would have been considerably greater, and consequently would most certainly have been accompanied by westward residential movement, had not Eaton's been unaffected by the fire. Indeed at this very period, Eaton's was expanding its operation adjacent to the Ward and so contributed to the stability of the area.

It was the Eaton strike of 1912 that fractured the artificial shell of inertia that had been maintaining the Ward for almost a decade. It came at a period of increased population and consequent overcrowding in the Ward; it came also at a time when economic expectations were rising among local Jews and when the confidence of the younger generation was coming to fruition. It propelled some Jewish employees into business for themselves, when perhaps otherwise they might have been content to remain. The municipal expropriations for the General Hospital and later for the Registry Office accelerated the process, as did the outbreak of the First World War, which gave new opportunities for contracts to smaller manufacturers, and unexpected profits to practitioners of the salvage trades, who suddenly found themselves in possession of quantities of scarce metals, glass and cloth. The "golden land" west of University Avenue now looked more inviting than ever and had at last entered the realm of reality. ❧

NOTES

1. J. E. Middleton, The Municipality of Toronto: A History (Toronto: Dominion Publishing Co., 1923), I, p. 402; C.S. Clark, *Of Toronto The Good* (Montreal: Toronto Publishing Co., 1898), p. 89.

2. Louis Rosenberg, *"Population Characteristics of the Jewish Community of Toronto"* (Montreal: Canadian Jewish Congress, 1955); Louis Rosenberg, *"Jewish Mutual Benefit and Friendly Societies in Toronto. The First Fifty Years 1896–1945"* (typescript, 63 pp., ca. 1947, Toronto Jewish Congress Archives).

3. See Bernard D. Weinryb, "Jewish Immigration and Accommodation to America" in M. Sklare, ed., *The Jews: Social Patterns of an American Group* (Glencoe, Ill.: Free Press, 1958).

4. J .B. Salsberg, personal interview, Jan. 15, 1973.

5. See Stephen A. Speisman, *The Jews of Toronto: A History to 1937* (Toronto: McClelland and Stewart, 1979), p. 73; and Maldwyn A. Jones, *American Immigration* (Chicago: University of Chicago Press, 1960), pp. 219-20.

6. For comparable patterns of ghetto formation, see David Ward, "The Emergence of Central Immigrant Ghettoes in American Cities: 1840–1920," Association of American Geographers, *Annals*, LVIII (June 1968), pp. 343-59; Moses Rischin, *The Promised City: New York's Jews, 1870–1914* (New York: Corinth Books, 1964); and Louis Wirth, *The Ghetto* (Chicago: University of Chicago Press, 1964), p. 202.

7. Samuel Charney, "From Rags to Riches," *Masada* IV, 2 (Oct. 1972), p. 11; David Green, personal interview Apr. 9, 1973; Ida Siegel, personal interview, Dec. 23, 1971. For sweatshop conditions in Montreal, see *The Jewish Times* (1903), p. 73.

8. Even when manufacturers engaged Jewish managers, as was the case with Sigmund Lubelsky at Eaton's, these were acculturated individuals with whom the East European Jew felt, often with justification, that he had little in common.

9. Weinryb, "Jewish Immigration," pp. 4-22; J. B. Salsberg, personal interview, Jan. 15, 1973; Harry Korolnek, personal interview, Dec. 26, 1972. For a contemporary description of Jewish occupations in the 1890s, see *Mail and Empire*, Sept. 25, 1897.

10. *Daily Star*, May 30, 1916.

11. See e.g., Charles N. Glaab and A. Theodore Brown, *A History of Urban America* (Toronto: Macmillan, 1967), p. 162.

12. Dr. Charles D. Hastings, "Report of the Medical Health Officer dealing with the recent investigation of Slum Conditions in Toronto 1911" (Toronto: Dept. of Health, n.d.; Folio No. 5, City of Toronto Archives).

13. One of these was Henry Greisman, a Galician manufacturer of suspenders. His houses were built as investment, not philanthropy, but he did rent them at a reasonable rate.

14. Hastings, *Report*, pp. 4, 8, 9, 12, 10-11.

15. See Canada, Bureau of Statistics, *Fifth Census of Canada*, 1911 (Ottawa, 1913) especially 11, p. 158; *Globe*, June 21, 1911; *Evening Telegram*, July 17, 1913.

16. Hastings, *Report*, pp. 5 ff.

17. See *Jewish Times*, Apr. 11, 1913, p. 28; Feb. 21, 1913, pp. 28-29; Sept. 6, 1912, p. 20; June 20, 1913.

18. Ibid., Dec. 14, 1906; Jan. 8, 1909.

19. S.B. Rohold, *The Jews in Canada* (Toronto: Board of Home Missions, Presbyterian Church in Canada, 1912), pp. 13-14.

20. See Assessment Role for City of Toronto made 1910 for 1911, Ward 3, Division II; Assessment Roll for City of Toronto made 1911 for 1912, Ward 4, Division II.

Opening of Eaton Centre Marks Passing of an Era

As I took my life in my hands trying to buy a pair of gloves at Eaton's final sale at the Queen Street store, I could not help being conscious that the opening of the new Eaton Centre would mark the passing of an age for Toronto Jews as well as for Eaton's itself. For it was on this site, in the Eaton factories, that many hundreds of Jewish immigrants found employment in the early years of this century.

But Eaton's factories are important not only because we worked there; they indirectly provided the impetus for the establishment of the Jewish-owned garment factories with which our community has so long been identified.

In some cities, especially those to which large numbers of German Jews came in the middle of the nineteenth century, the manufacture of clothing was often in Jewish hands from the outset. In other cities, where East Europeans made up the bulk of the Jewish population at an early date, the Jewish role tended to be that of labourer, and only upheaval within the industry propelled Jews into the establishment of their own factories.

Occasionally, this took the form of a depression which forced

From The Canadian Jewish News, February 18, 1977.

165

View of T. Eaton Company factories, May 1919. Eaton's employed as many as 1,200 tailors mostly Jewish men and women. After the long and bitter strike against Eaton's in 1912, many Jewish tailors went into business for themselves.

large firms into bankruptcy and allowed newcomers to purchase existing plants cheaply; in other instances, changes in the railway network deprived factories of their market and shifted the advantage to others. The most common disturbance, however, was labour unrest, and strikes, more often lost than won, encouraged Jewish workmen to venture out on their own. The pattern was similar across North America, but in Toronto the turning point was the Eaton strike of 1912.

Jews from Eastern Europe arrived in Toronto by the thousands immediately prior to the First World War. Finding their traditional skills useless, they gravitated to the factories in a city fast becoming a centre for light manufacturing, especially clothing. Bay Street, Wellington and the neighbouring thoroughfares abounded with plants for the manufacture of men's and women's garments, the principal being Johnson Brothers and the Lowndes Company. But farther north, the T. Eaton Company was rapidly becoming the largest single employer of "operators."

Eaton's, already well known as a retail establishment, had branched out into the mail-order field late in the nineteenth century. Supplies of goods were undependable, however, and middle-men were costly; consequently, by 1900, Eaton's was contemplating the manufacture of its own goods for this market.

Although the company acquired factories for a variety of items ranging from stoves to shoes, those in Toronto concentrated primarily on the manufacture of underwear, men's suits and women's apparel. By 1907 a complex of buildings had been built for this purpose in the blocks bounded by James, Teraulay (now Bay), Alice (later Teraulay and now obliterated by the Eaton Centre) and Albert Streets, and it was here that as many as 1,200 recently-arrived Jews were earning their livelihood by 1912.

Those employed in the manufacture of clothing at Eaton's were not exclusively Jewish; indeed, Irish girls and Italians made up a large proportion of the work force. Jews, however, constituted a substantial majority. Eaton's was especially popular because of its proximity to "the Ward," where most of the city's Jews then resided.

For a decade, local intellectuals had been agitating for the organization of unions in the garment factories, and if this task was difficult elsewhere, it was especially awesome at Eaton's. For one thing, most agreed that working conditions here were not bad, especially when compared to those in the larger cities in the United States, notably New York with its infamous Lower East Side sweatshops. Besides, most workers were too happy to have jobs of any sort, enhancing the prospect of bringing their families from Europe, to concern themselves with bargaining with their employers.

Nevertheless, wages were low and unrest was on the increase. There were charges that Eaton's attempted to determine the minimum upon which their employees could survive, in order to keep salaries as low as possible. Other complaints concerned the lack of cleanliness and privacy in the shops. The problem was to convince the labourer that conditions could be improved only through the introduction of a union.

By 1910, the strength of the garment workers' unions in the United States had been augmented considerably by concessions gained from employers following a number of strikes in New York. Encouraged, these unions—the Amalgamated in the field of men's

clothing and the International Ladies' Garment Workers' Union (ILGWU) in women's—sent off agents to other centres in the hope of achieving similar successes. Since a preponderance of those employed in the garment trades were Jews, the union organizers, too, tended to be Jewish and had the advantage of being able to communicate with prospective unionists in Yiddish.

By 1912 several of these American organizers were active in the larger Canadian cities, and in Toronto they came just in time to infuse new vigour into the efforts of local unionists. It appears that the latter had at last persuaded isolated groups of workers to strike against some of the smaller plants and had succeeded in wringing a few insignificant concessions from them. However, all were encouraged and prepared to attack the largest "culprit," Eaton's.

This enthusiasm coincided with a new company policy of forcing employees to produce extra garments in the slow season

168

Horse-drawn delivery wagons stream out from the T. Eaton Company to every corner of the growing city in this ad from the Toronto Star, 1907.

in preparation for busy times. The added pressure, needless to say, was extremely unpopular and provided just the pretext the union organizers needed to grind operations to a halt.

Most of the Jewish workers, who were employed primarily in those departments affected by the walkout, were bewildered by these developments. The whole experience of defiance was foreign to them and many, however displeased they may have been with working conditions, were not anxious to have their only source of income cut off. Few had saved any money to speak of, and the unions had neither the financial resources nor the inclination to subsidize them.

The strike dragged on for twelve agonizing weeks and although it never did become identified in the public mind as an exclusively Jewish issue, the Jewish community in Toronto was profoundly affected since most of the strikers were Jews. Local Jewish women attempted to collect funds in the streets to support the strikers' families, but the municipal authorities declared the practice illegal. A recently-organized association of Jewish charities, consisting principally of women's organizations, did what it could to offer relief in the form of groceries, clothing and grants of money, but this proved far from adequate.

Labour elements, however, capitalized on the disturbance. The ILGWU, United States-based as it was, held its annual convention in Toronto to demonstrate support for the strikers, while the Toronto

169

Trades and Labour Council, an association of local workers' organizations, urged its members to support the Eaton workers since any gains they might make would surely benefit everyone.

In the meantime, efforts were under way to persuade employer and employee to come to terms. Even the mayor attempted to mediate. Eaton's, however, refused to retreat. John Craig Eaton, president of the company since the death of his father, Timothy, five years earlier, had prided himself in carrying on the family tradition of benevolent paternalism towards employees.

The Eaton firm had, indeed, initiated shorter working hours, company-sponsored welfare plans, camps and numerous other features, but these touched the English-speaking sales staff more than it did the factory operatives. Nevertheless, Eaton considered the strike nothing less than evidence of ingratitude on the part of his employees and an affront to the family. His position was that he was willing to forgive and forget, but that the strikers must return penitent and without condition.

Efforts in behalf of the strikers, both from within the Jewish community and outside it, were fruitless and although at the end of twelve weeks of sporadic negotiation there were hints that Eaton's might be willing to discuss improvements in working conditions after an end to the strike, in reality, the strikers had gained nothing. Time was on the side of the company; the workers were literally starved into submission and most returned to the shops despondent and much poorer. Indeed, so severe a blow was the failure of the Eaton strike that the development of unionism in Toronto was set back almost ten years.

The strike, however, was not without favourable consequences for local Jews, although these were to become evident only in the ensuing decades. Its immediate effect was to channel the more independent and ambitious Eaton employees into manufacturing ventures of their own.

If the aim of these new Jewish establishments was to drive Eaton's out of the field, they were far from successful. The larger firm had the advantage in the market by weight of sheer volume production. Gradually, the Jewish factories abandoned efforts to produce complete garments, except perhaps for those making shirts and trousers. For the most part, they concentrated on specialized items: suspenders, buttons and button holes, sleeves and collars, developing into an ancillary service for the larger non-Jewish firms, including Eaton's.

Within the next decade, it became evident that in this area the large firms were at a disadvantage. The new Jewish factories were able to produce far more cheaply than the older firms because of the nature of their labour force. The Jewish manufacturer tended to employ Jews exclusively, these often being his relatives or at least recently arrived *landsleit*.

The latter, insecure in their new environment, preferred Jewish employers to Gentile, even at lower wages. This, incidentally, was especially true of those who were *shomrei Shabbat*, since most non-Jewish factories opened on Saturday mornings during the busy season. As a result, the larger firms soon realized that it was more economical to contract work out to the Jewish manufacturers than to maintain their own factories.

Assistance from this quarter enabled Jewish firms in Toronto to survive and even to prosper. Only a few, however, would have established themselves independently in the first place had it not been for labour unrest and in particular the Eaton strike. ❧

Above, Brown's illustration of the proposed Beth Jacob, the 'Henry Street' or 'Poilisher Shul,' 1921. The domes were evidently scaled back and the large circular 'rose-window' altered. From Canadian Jewish Review, Dec. 9, 1921. Below, Beth Jacob in May 1965, shortly before the building was sold. (Speisman)

172

View of Primrose Club in final stage of construction; note unfinished verandahs. Located on Willcocks Street east of Spadina, Primrose operated as an upscale Jewish social club for decades. The building now houses the University of Toronto Faculty Club. Photo from Canadian Jewish Review, December 1921.

Architect Benjamin Brown—An Appreciation

MOST JEWS WHO HAVE LIVED in Toronto for any length of time consider the Henry Street Shul, the Brunswick Talmud Torah, the old Primrose Club on Willcocks Street, the Standard Yiddish Theatre and a host of industrial buildings on lower Spadina Avenue landmarks of our community. Few, however, associate those structures with their designer, Benjamin Brown.

Brown was a man of creativity and taste, an artist who had the distinction of being the first Jewish graduate architect to practice in Toronto. Avoiding the public eye, he lived in virtual obscurity and when he died last December [1974] at the age of eighty-seven, few aside from his family and immediate circle of acquaintances took note at the passing of a pioneer.

From the Canadian Jewish News, February 7, 1975.

Air!
Space!
Light!

. . . . . The New
Hermant Building

TAKING its place on Toronto's skyline as one of the finest and most up-to-date creations in modern architecture. The following brief outline of the new 15-story Hermant Building is worthy of note. Actual work commenced on July 13th, 1929, when the wreckers proceeded to demolish an old five-story building which stood on the site. On September 4th the first concrete was poured in the forms—109 days after, the roof was placed on this beautiful building. Constructed of reinforced concrete, strictly fireproof, and modern in every respect—lightest offices in the city, with a beautiful and spacious marble entrance, offices will be ready for occupancy March 1st.

The Wilton Construction Company, under the supervision of John Hagerty, are responsible for the erection of this modern office home.

AREA—Floors available in following areas: 12,000 feet to a floor; 6,000 feet to a floor; 4,500 feet to a floor; or divided to suit tenant.

THE Turnbull Elevator Co. of Toronto were responsible for the installation of elevators. 300 to 400 people per minute can be taken care of on the two passenger elevators equipped with variable voltage controls. Separate motor generators are provided to operate each elevator. Control system will be the Turnbull Westinghouse.

Spacious freight elevators are also provided to take care of the various needs of the tenants.

BENJAMIN BROWN, Architect

H. C. LEFROY, Structural Engineer

322 Federal Building — Waverley 3304

For Reservations Apply Hermant Building, 21 Dundas Square, at Yonge — Tel. WA. 2159

Advertisement for Hermant Building showing Brown's 15-storey tower beside original nine-storey structure, describing its modern conveniences and innovations. Toronto Star, January 31, 1930. Photo at left is circa 1950.

174

Above, Brown family portrait, Toronto, 1901, shows Meyer and Tema Brown and children Manny, Sophie, Peter and Benjamin (upper right). Photo at right shows the architect in his later years.

Benjamin Brown arrived in Toronto from "White Russia" at the age of eleven late in the nineteenth century and spent the early years of his life here in a rear cottage on Elizabeth Street. His parents, like so many Jewish immigrants of the period, were not affluent people and by the time he had his bar mitzvah, Brown had been forced to cut short his education in order to help support his family. Many in similar circumstances became newsboys, but young Ben found a position as a messenger for his uncle, a tailor. Before long he had entered a readymade clothing factory as an apprentice operator.

The shop abounded with young Jews, some of whom planned to find a career in the industry, but there were also a number who sought employment in the factories merely to finance their university educations. Through these, Brown was drawn into the Nordau Zion Club, where he met additional students and became imbued with a desire to continue his own studies.

At first he attended the Ontario School of Art, then located over the Princess Theatre on King Street. His intention was to become a painter, but he soon discovered an artist's education would have to include European experience, something for which

Balfour Building, ca 1930; and elegantly arched doorway of same, 2012. Note the disguised water tower on the roof. The building is considered one of the landmarks of Spadina Avenue.

money simply was not available in the Brown household. As a result, in order to combine artistry with a practical means of earning a living, Brown resolved to pursue a career in architecture. The question was how to gain admittance to a university without even a completed elementary education let alone graduation from high school.

Fortunately, Brown had the determination to study for his matriculation in his spare time, despite the skepticism of his father who believed the hurdle was insurmountable. He was assisted by his friends in the Nordau Zion Club, many of whom were medical students. Dr. M. A. Pollock, who had been his instructor as an operator in the factory, tutored him in English grammar; Dr. L. G. Solway in composition and history; Dr. Pivnik in geometry and algebra. French and German he learned on his own and, with his successful matriculation, he entered the University of Toronto. The other members of his family, now convinced of his ability, went to work to finance his education, and in 1919 he graduated as an architect.

176

A year of experience in New York and Philadelphia enabled him to open a practice in Toronto, accepting small assignments from an exclusively Jewish clientele. His first commission, a row of ten terrace houses at the corner of Beverley Street and Grange Avenue, done for a Mr. Rabinowitch, a rag peddler who had become a real estate developer, is still standing. The same is true of an apartment block on Queen Street, in Parkdale, built for Mr. Garfunkel the *shoichet*. By late 1921 Brown was concentrating on commercial and industrial structures: a small bakery on Agnes Street (now Dundas), a factory for Empire Clothing (now the Schiffer–Hillman building) on Spadina Avenue, an addition to Percy Hermant's Imperial Optical (Hermant Building) at Dundas Square and Victoria.

The following year he began work on the building for which he best deserves recognition. Brown's commission to design the Beth Jacob Synagogue ("Poilisher Shul") on Henry Street would result in one of Toronto's architectural gems and certainly the most sensitive synagogue composition in the city.

The building was a triumph, with a hall seating 800 people, capped by five domes which made its acoustics remarkable. There was also a spacious *beth midrash*, a mikvah and an apartment for the *shammes*. Brown even designed the interior furnishings and the Aron Kodesh which can still be seen in the new Beth Jacob on Overbrook Place in Downsview.

Brown's Primrose Club, now the Faculty Club at the University of Toronto, was designed along the lines of an English men's club and more particularly, on the model of the National Club building on Bay Street. As for the Talmud Torah, he was able to combine in one building—then considered one of the most modern of its type on this continent—classrooms as well fitted out as those in the public schools, an auditorium, a chapel, catering and athletic facilities. At his suggestion, the board of the Talmud Torah inspected Jewish educational buildings in several American cities before deciding upon a design for their own.

A notable feature of Brown's industrial buildings is the apparent absence of the ugly water tanks on the roofs. Actually, these are

177

Right, Brown's fine drawing of the Brunswick Avenue Talmud Torah from 'The Jew in Canada,' 1926. He also designed the Gelber Textile Building, centre, ca 1920s; the illustration is again from 'The Jew in Canada.' At left is an illustration of the companion building to the Gelber Textile Building on Richmond Street West; architect unknown. From Gelber Brothers Ltd. letterhead, 1925.

present since fire regulations require them, but if the reader looks at the Balfour Building, for instance, at the corner of Spadina and Adelaide, he will notice the tank enclosed in a brick tower. Brown was one of the first architects to insist upon this device, a good fifty years before Torontonians became conscious of the need to consider how this city ought to look.

Ben Brown seldom received the recognition that he deserved, nor the material rewards often associated with the profession. But at least once in recent years we did allow him a little *nachas* from his art. Last June, when the archives committee of the Canadian Jewish Congress conducted tours of the Kensington Market area, we invited him to be our guest and had the pleasure of introducing him to the community during the event. Maybe those who did not have the chance to applaud him then might take a stroll down Henry Street or down Spadina Avenue in his memory.

Rabbi Levy was invited to the pulpit of Shomrei Shabbos, the Galicianer (Austrian) Synagogue on Chestnut Street, in 1906, shortly after half the congregation had departed to start a new congregation and build a new shul on Teraulay Street. Above view of Shomrei Shabbos, ca 1900–10. For a much later photograph, see page 44.

The Saga of Rabbi Meyer Zvi Levy

ONE OF THE CHARACTERISTICS of rabbinical careers in North America in the early part of this century, and perhaps even today, is the frequency with which individuals relocate from one city to another. For a rabbi to stay in one place for a decade or twenty years was a rarity, but to be a part of a single community for a half-century was simply remarkable.

Rabbi Meyer Zvi Levy, whose twenty-fifth *yahrzeit* is observed this week, was one of those unusual men—one who not only set down roots in this community but had a continuing impact on it during his lifetime as well. For unlike many rabbis of his period, who isolated themselves within their own synagogues and their particular ethnic communities, Rabbi Levy saw Toronto Jewry as a single entity, and he was comfortable in every corner of it.

From the Canadian Jewish News, March 12, 1981.

Photograph of interior of Shomrei Shabbos, Chestnut Street, from Canadian Jewish Times, 1899; the building was a former church. Opposite, Rabbi Meyer Zvi Levy, ca 1930s, from 'Canadian Jewry: Prominent Jews of Canada,' 1933.

Born in 1871 in the village of Yagustov, Russian Poland, Levy studied as a child at the yeshiva of Suvalk and shortly after becoming bar mitzvah, sat for admission to the great yeshiva of Volozhin, Lithuania, where he attracted the approval of the renowned Rabbi Chaim Soloveitchik.

At the age of eighteen he accepted the position of chazzan in his home town, but after a year, during which he married, he returned to Lithuania, this time to Eisheshok near Vilna, to continue his studies. Finally, in 1891, he received *smicha* (ordination) from Rabbi Shlomo Yisroel Moshe Cohen of Vilna and from the chief of the *beth din* of Eisheshok, Rabbi Tzvi Hersh.

At the age of twenty-two, however, prepared to embark upon a rabbinical career, Meyer Levy was conscripted into the Russian army. The Czarist regime had just embarked upon a series of foreign wars designed to bring glory to Russia, but which would culminate in the disastrous Russo-Japanese War of 1904–5. Like many other young Jews in the same situation, Levy resolved to emigrate.

His yeshiva connections in Europe gave him introduction to Rabbi Jacob Joseph, then Chief Rabbi of New York, and it was with

Rabbi Joseph that he stayed after his arrival in the United States. Emigration also resulted in a change of name. His original family name of "Yosefsky" was changed to "Levy" to save a US immigration official the trouble of spelling it. After a few months, Rabbi Joseph's glowing recommendation secured him a post in Syracuse, where he remained until 1897.

Rabbi Levy took his role seriously, and when complicated *halakhic* questions arose, he did not hesitate to correspond with the principal authorities in the field, including Rabbi Isaac Elchonon Spektor of Kovno. Nevertheless, he began to find the role of an American congregational rabbi distasteful and he decided to try his hand at commerce.

His trade ventures took him first to Rochester, then Detroit, but by 1906, after several years of success, the bottom fell out of his business. As Rabbi Levy told it himself, "I lost all my possessions, and barely had anything left with which to feed my household. I then began to believe that God doesn't want me to be in the business field, but rather to return to . . . the calling of the rabbinate, even though I didn't want it."

The story is told, perhaps apocryphally, that during his stay in Detroit Levy became acquainted with Henry Ford who was then attempting to borrow money to build automobiles. When Ford approached him for a loan, Levy, like everyone else, considered the eccentric a poor risk and declined what might even have become a partnership.

In any case, at this point, an upheaval had taken place in the Chestnut Street synagogue of the Galician Jews in Toronto— so serious that the congregations split. The secessionists formed a new congregation on Teraulay Street and Rabbi Weinreb, who was then rabbi of the Galician community, went with them. The older congregation, Shomrei Shabbos, now invited Rabbi Levy to its pulpit.

Over the next fifty years in Toronto, Meyer Levy would serve a number of local congregation including the Russisher Shul (Shaarei Tzedek), the Romainisher Shul (Adath Israel) and finally, for many

Rabbi Levy worked with Canadian Jewish Congress to organize and participate in a protest rally against the Nazi persecution of Jews soon after Kristalnacht. It filled Maple Leaf Gardens to the rafters. Toronto Star, November 21, 1938.

years, the Hebrew Men of England which, by the 1930s was one of the largest synagogues in the city. (He also had brief associations with the Minsker Synagogue and the Palmerston Avenue Shul.)

Rabbi Levy immediately plunged himself into the communal life of the city, indeed of the province. Prior to the First World War he participated with the other rabbis in the operation of a *Vaad Hakashrut* to ensure the proper supply of kosher products, and later took an active part in the *Kehillah* of Toronto. By the late 1940s, as the senior rabbi of the city, he was president of the Rabbinical Council (*Vaad Harabonim*) of Toronto.

But Levy saw his role as rabbi as extending beyond the areas of congregational life and ritual observance.

His prescription for Jewish survival included the enhancement of broad Jewish culture, and the establishment of peaceful relations among Jews and between Jews and the non-Jewish community. Consequently, he was active in the founding of a local Yiddish newspaper, the *Hebrew Journal*, in 1912; a lifelong Zionist, he was a Toronto delegate to the Canadian Zionist convention in Ottawa the same year; he traveled throughout the province, accepting invitations to dedicate newly-built synagogues, especially in the Niagara peninsula; he visited Jewish prisoners at Kingston Penitentiary and provincial correctional facilities on a regular basis, and at times appeared in court to plead for clemency for Jewish criminals.

Rabbi Levy even donated a *T'nach* to the municipal courts, so that Jews would not have to be sworn on a Christian bible.

1 SUPERINTENDENT
2 TREASURER
3 HOUSE COMMITTEE
4
5 NURSE

Remember us and God will
remember you.

פֿאַרגעסט ניט אין אונז אלטיטישטע
וועם גאָט אין אייך ניט פֿערגעסען

Rabbi Levy devoted himself in his later years to raising funds for the Jewish Old Folks Home on Cecil Street. The photo shows some staff and residents gathered in front of the Home, ca 1930s.

Rabbi Levy was a true proponent of *ahavat Yisrael*; his concern for Jews extended from the domestic to the international, from the personal to the communal. At home, he worked to overcome the opposition of financial and commercial institutions to the hiring of Jews, and had real success with the Toronto General Trusts, Simpsons and the Toronto *Star*. He was even able to secure jobs for a few with the provincial government.

As early as 1923, he persuaded the University of Toronto to permit Sabbath-observing Jewish students to write alternate examinations, and influenced a similar decision at McGill in Montreal.

On the international scene, Rabbi Levy, prominent among the local Orthodox rabbinate, worked with Canadian Jewish Congress in the protest meeting against Nazism which took place at Maple Leaf Gardens following Kristalnacht in 1938.

On an individual basis, while some rabbis found a supplementary source of income by arranging divorces, Levy's approach was to exhaust all possibilities in reconciling the couple. On the communal level, he maintained cordial relationships with rabbis serving Reform and Conservative congregations.

The period during which he served Toronto was not one in which rabbis were highly paid and it was extremely difficult for a man of his integrity to raise a large family on the meager earnings to be had in the rabbinate. Consequently, Rabbi Levy—in the ancient rabbinical tradition always reluctant to make a living from Torah—made and sold kosher wine (he got a special permit to do so during Prohibition) and he became the local agent for the B. Manischewitz Company. To those who knew and understood the man—and indeed Jewish values—these activities never detracted from Rabbi Levy's stature and dignity.

Rabbi Levy and the Rebbitzen as well were perhaps best known for their work for the Jewish Old Folks Home. Rabbi Levy traveled throughout the province to raise money for it and he occupied an honoured position at the groundbreaking ceremonies for the new Baycrest facility.

His death in February of 1956 brought to an end a career of service seldom paralleled in North American Jewry and one for which this community ought to honour his memory. ৩

Scene from Ossip Dymow's 'The Eternal Wanderer,' one of Thomashefsky's famous productions. National Theatre, New York, 1913. Local entrepreneurs imported many New York Yiddish productions to Toronto.

Yiddish Theatre in Toronto

THE NINETEENTH CENTURY SAW the gradual disintegration of the homogeneity of East European Jewish *shtetl* society and the emergence of a secular Yiddish culture. Theatre was one expression of this phenomenon in larger urban centres. With large-scale immigration to the United States, the Yiddish theatre, too, found fertile ground, eventually coming to full fruition on Second Avenue in New York City.

Productions varied in origin and tone. Some were adaptations of English or Russian classics; Shakespeare was especially popular. Others were written specifically for the Yiddish stage. Comedies abounded, but the tragedy was the hallmark of Yiddish drama. Like most other aspects of Yiddish culture in Canada, Toronto Yiddish theatre was dominated largely by the United States. Nevertheless, one of the earliest attempts at the establishment of a local Yiddish theatre was an indigenous one.

From Polyphony: The Journal of the Multicultural History Society of Ontario, Vol. 5, No. 2, Fall/Winter 1983.

Lyric Theatre, northeast corner Agnes and Teraulay (Dundas and Bay) in WWI era. Built 1860 as a Methodist church, the building was home to Yiddish theatre for more than a decade. Later it was called the National; a few Chinese plays were also performed on its stage. It was demolished 1924 after a damaging fire.

In 1906 two individuals named Michaelson and Abramov attempted to open a theatre on Elizabeth Street in the Ward. Michaelson operated an ice-cream parlour in the area and Abramov was a self-styled actor and director who probably made his living in a more practical manner. Together with Abramov's wife, they formed a theatrical company, but their efforts quickly met with failure. It became apparent that Yiddish theatre would be practical only if local impresarios imported American companies. Granted, this had been tried without success as early as 1897, when a group of Jewish actors from the United States opened a theatre in a vacant church on Richmond Street. However, the number of Yiddish-speaking Jews in Toronto was still too small to support it, while the English-speaking Jews of the established community and the children of East European immigrants understood too little Yiddish to appreciate the linguistic nuances or the allusions dependent upon the European experience. The Orthodox, moreover, considered the Yiddish theatre irreligious and consequently ignored it.

186

Ad for Lyric Theatre from Canadian Jewish Times, ca 1912. Below, photo of theatre entrepreneur Charles Pasternak, from Keneder Adler, 1913.

During the following decade, however, things began to change. The Jewish population grew and diversified and began to include more of those who had experienced Yiddish theatre in the United States or in the larger East European cities. In addition, the number of secularist Jews had increased, while the religious were becoming more tolerant. The growing popularity of the Yiddish theatre was not surprising, for it served an important psychological function for the Jewish immigrant. Here he could find relaxation after a day at the factory, rise out of the indignity of his existence as a rag-picker, or the drudgery of domestic routine to heights attainable only in fantasy. Here, also, there was catharsis: no matter how much *tzores* (trouble) one had, the character on the stage always had more.

The first successful Yiddish theatre in Toronto was due to the efforts of a local entrepreneur, Charles Pasternak. Opened in 1906 and named the People's Theatre, it was housed in the former Lithuanian synagogue at University Avenue and Elm Street. The People's drew a few local artists but it functioned primarily by means of American touring companies, which were glad to have an alternative to the Orange Hall at Queen and Berti Streets where distance from the Ward had seriously diminished attendance. Success was not immediate. Perhaps the People's Theatre acquired

187

The marquee and sidewalk in front of the Standard Yiddish Theatre are visible in this view of the east side of Spadina Avenue, north from Dundas Street, 1930.

an unfavourable reputation after its balcony almost collapsed at one performance and the men in the audience had to hold it up while its occupants made their escape. Nonetheless, the theatre did survive and Yiddish theatre, generally, grew more popular. Benefit performances in aid of various organizations became almost commonplace and were well attended. For example, when the local Zionists brought Jacob Adler's renowned company from New York in 1909, two thousand people filled Massey Hall, which had been engaged for the event. Indeed, Massey Hall was the venue for most of the great New York companies that visited Toronto.

That same year Pasternak and a partner acquired the Methodist church building at Agnes and Teraulay (Dundas and Bay) Streets and moved the People's Theatre into the new premises. Renamed the Lyric and later the National, after New York houses, it packed in the audience "to the very doors."

Instead of operating it himself, Pasternak adopted the practice of leasing the Lyric to various American managers and over the next decade a variety of entertainment, ranging from the New York Yiddish Opera to high-quality dramas, was provided, and capacity audiences were the rule during the season between September and May. But the frequency with which the lease changed hands suggests that Yiddish theatre was not really a profitable venture in Toronto.

Ad for 'Matkes Khasene' ('Matkes's Wedding') starring Julius Natanson at Standard Theatre, Hebrew Journal, 1931. After years of declining attendance, the Standard became the Strand movie house in 1935. It became the Victory Theatre about 1941 and was later transformed into the storied Victory Burlesque.

By the early 1920s the Ward was no longer sufficiently Jewish to warrant continued operation of the Lyric. In fact, the management had been reduced to renting it for boxing matches. By this time, however, a new syndicate, including Pasternak and Isidore Axler, was building a grand new theatre in the heart of the new Jewish area at Spadina Avenue and Dundas Street. The Standard Theatre was the first in Canada to be built as a Yiddish playhouse, and it accommodated 1,200 people. Its success, after its opening in August 1922, was immediate—a phenomenon due in large measure to its manager, Abe Littman. An individual of wide experience, Littman had worked in a variety of American centres and even for a time at the Lyric. During the two years that he managed the Standard, Littman operated one of the finest Yiddish theatrical companies on the continent. Indeed, the Toronto company played Cleveland, St. Louis, Chicago and Detroit, and even performed regularly in New York.

In 1924 Littman was enticed to Detroit and his departure

189

signaled a decline for the Standard Theatre. The local company struggled on for a while but was eventually supplanted by visiting troupes from New York. By the mid-1930s the advent of radio and sound motion pictures, coupled with the growing acculturation of the second-generation immigrants, dealt the Standard a final blow. By 1935 the Strand, as it was now called, had become a movie house.

The demise of the Standard did not, however, eliminate Yiddish performances in Toronto. Touring companies still played at Massey Hall and at Alhambra Hall on Spadina Avenue, but their appearances became more and more sporadic, and increasingly they came to be sponsored by local organizations attempting to raise funds. Local professional companies, often consisting of actors who earned their livelihoods at some other occupation, sprang up and disappeared with regularity, and by the outbreak of World War Two, the survival of live Yiddish theatre in Toronto rested largely in the hands of amateur troupes, often associated with mutual benefit organizations such as the Arbeiter Ring or the Labour League. Yiddish variety shows had greater longevity, but they, too, fell victim to radio and film.

Recent decades have seen a renewed interest in Yiddish theatre, but an attempt to establish a professional company in Toronto in the mid-1970s was unrealistic. Yiddish theatre today remains the preserve of the amateur and the part-time professional, a trend that will probably remain constant. ☙

Jones Avenue—Toronto's Second Jewish Cemetery

A CENTURY AGO, MARTIN MCKEE and his wife Margaret came into possession of a parcel of land on the western outskirts of the village of Leslieville, Ontario. In all probability they had inherited it from deceased relatives, and McKee, a small-town merchant, had little interest in farming it. Besides the area was too hilly to be cultivated easily.

Nor was he attracted by the prospect of holding his property for speculation. Granted, the surrounding area had recently seceded from Leslieville and had established itself as the new village of Riverdale. Moreover, a dirt road had been laid out past his lots and named Clifford Street. But land was not selling; it was considered too far from any outpost of civilization to be commercially valuable. To McKee's mind, nothing would come of the grandiose scheme for development and he resolved to rid himself of the land while it was still saleable.

In the spring of 1883 these circumstances could not have been more auspicious for a small group of East European Jews recently arrived in Toronto. They had just founded the city's second Jewish congregation, soon to be named Goel Tzedec, and although they were still without a permanent place of worship, they were busy

From the Beth Tzedec Bulletin, 1975

191

Left, kever or grave site of Rabbi Yosef Weinreb, the 'Galicianer Rav,' in Jones Avenue Cemetery. Right, view of terraced rows of tombstones on the cemetery's sloped terrain.

with what they considered an even greater priority, the acquisition of a *bais oylom*, a cemetery.

Toronto had had a Jewish burial ground for almost forty years, but it belonged to Holy Blossom, the congregation of the established and acculturated Jews. The newcomers wanted a place of their own, where the *minhagim* [customs] of their own districts in Russia and Lithuania could be followed without interference or objection.

In typical Jewish fashion, the new congregation appointed a committee to search for a piece of land. The purchase was not to be put off, for although most of these immigrants were relatively young, fatal disease might strike at any time and infant and child-bed mortality was high. Moreover, many hoped before long to bring elderly parents from Europe and the reality of human frailty had to be faced.

Few, if any, of the immigrants were wealthy, but the congregation chose for this task a group of men who had not only shown some leadership in the establishment of the new synagogue but, more importantly, were known for their relative success in business. Among them one finds such individuals as Yaakov Draimin (for many years head of the *chevra kadisha* at Goel Tzedec), David Garavsky (Gurofsky) and Benjamin Yanover, whose descendants were to play prominent roles in the life of this community.

The means by which these Jews made contact with the McKees will probably remain forever lost to history. No congregational records of this period now exist. However, money was not plentiful

192

and land in the city proper was expensive. Admittedly, a number of Christian churches had cemeteries in Toronto itself, or just north of it—the city then extended only a little north of Bloor Street—but these had been acquired in the middle of the nineteenth century or earlier and some had been granted by the Crown as part of the Clergy Reserves, lots set aside for use by Christian religious groups. Land close to the city was now far too expensive. Besides, the municipal authorities were by this time beginning to regard the establishment of new burial grounds within city boundaries with disfavour; it would hamper residential and commercial development, and Toronto Jews had too little influence at City Hall to make them change their minds. There was little choice, therefore, but to find a site outside the city.

The area east of Toronto, and Leslieville in particular, was already familiar to local Jewry; the old Jewish cemetery was located there. Consequently, it is not surprising that land was sought in that direction. The purchase on Clifford Avenue, later renamed Jones Avenue in honour of John Jones, the city engineer, was concluded for the princely sum of $135 "lawful money of Canada," just after Pesach.

The new burial ground exhibited a significant difference from the older cemetery on what is now Pape Avenue. The latter, despite the fact that it would continue to be used for another half-century, was marshy and burials were often dependent upon the weather. The Goel Tzedec property, however, was on high ground, the very feature that had made it unattractive for farming, and so was completely untroubled by such difficulty, although the sheer incline of the hill on its western side would eventually require the construction of retaining terraces to prevent erosion.

Another contrast with Pape Avenue had to do with the attitude of the congregants at Goel Tzedec more than with the lay of the land. The old cemetery had been enclosed, but originally only by a simple picket fence, to prevent entry by stray animals and by children. The members of Holy Blossom, English and Central European as they were, appeared to have had little fear of vandalism.

At Jones Avenue, by contrast, the burial ground became a veritable fortress, surrounded by enormous, forbidding walls. The Russian and Lithuanian Jews of Goel Tzedec, and the Galicians who purchased the adjacent lot for a cemetery in the 1890s, had had too much experience with grave desecration in Europe to leave their dead unprotected. When the two organizations cooperated to erect the walls in 1918–1919, the style chosen was a church-like Gothic, devoid of Jewish markings except for a *magen david* over each of the entrances, almost as if to disguise the nature of the property.

In our own time, there are few burials at Jones Avenue. After the amalgamation of the University Avenue and McCaul Street synagogues, Beth Tzedec preferred the latter's Dawes Road cemetery, while the opening of the new Beth Tzedec Memorial Park on Bathurst Street above Finch Avenue further discouraged use of the congregation's original burial ground.

But the fortress remains, its original brick now stuccoed and painted a striking white, a solemn reminder of the congregation's pioneers who lie buried there and of the insecurity which one would hope has largely been absent from the experience of their descendants.

Select Bibliography

— *What is "the Ward" going to do with Toronto?: a report on undesirable living conditions in one section of the city of Toronto—"the Ward"—conditions which are spreading rapidly to other districts.* Toronto: Bureau of Municipal Research, ca 1918.

— *Yoyvl bukh: 25 yoriger yubiley Talmud Torah Ets Hayim.* (Jubilee Book published on the 25th anniversary of the Eitz Chaim Talmud Torah, D'Arcy Street; mostly Yiddish.) Toronto: published privately, 1943.

Abella, Irving. *A Coat of Many Colours: Two centuries of Jewish life in Canada.* Toronto: Key Porter, 1990.

Abella, Irving; Goodman, Edwin; and Sharp, Rosalie, eds. *Growing Up Jewish, Canadians tell their own stories.* Toronto: McClelland & Stewart, 1997.

Abella, Irving and Troper, Harold. *None Is Too Many: Canada and the Jews of Europe, 1933-1948.* Toronto: Lester & Orpen Dennys, 1982.

Culiner, Jill. *Finding Home: in the footsteps of the Jewish fusgeyers.* Toronto: Sumach Press, 2004.

Eisen, David. *Diary of a Medical Student.* Toronto: Canadian Jewish Congress, 1974.

Eisendrath, Maurice N. *Can Faith Survive? the thoughts and afterthoughts of an American rabbi.* New York: McGraw-Hill, 1964.

Gladstone, Bill. *The Story of Beth Lida Forest Hill Congregation: a Toronto synagogue's first century (1912–2012).* Toronto: Now and Then Books, 2012.

Goldbloom, Alton. *Small Patients: the autobiography of a children's doctor.* Toronto: Longmans Green, 1959.

Harney, Robert F. and Troper, Harold. *Immigrants: A portrait of the urban experience, 1890–1930.* Toronto: Van Nostrand Reinhold, 1975.

Hart, Arthur Daniel (ed). *The Jew in Canada: a complete record of Canadian Jewry from the days of the French Regime to the present time.* Toronto: Jewish Publications, 1926. (Abridged facsimile edition published by Now and Then Books, Toronto 2011.)

Kage, Joseph. *With Faith and Thanksgiving: the story of two hundred years of Jewish immigration and immigrant aid effort in Canada (1760–1960).* Montreal: Eagle Publishing Company, 1962.

Kayfetz, Benjamin. "Growing Up on Dundas Street." From Abella, Irving et al, *Growing Up Jewish (op cit.)*

Kayfetz, Benjamin. "My Life at Cheder." From *Polyphony: Bulletin of the Multicultural History Society of Ontario*, vol. II, 1989.

Levendal, Louis. *A Century of the Canadian Jewish Press, 1880s–1980s.* Ottawa: Borealis Press, 1989.

Levitt, Cyril H., and Shaffir, William. *The Riot at Christie Pits.* Toronto: Lester & Orpen Dennys, 1987.

Lipinsky, Jack. *Imposing Their Will: an organizational history of Jewish Toronto, 1933-1948.* Montreal: McGill-Queen's University Press, 2011.

Luftspring, Sammy; with Brian Swarbrick. *Call Me Sammy.* Toronto: Prentice-Hall of Canada, 1975.

Mendelson, Alan. *Exiles from Nowhere: the Jews and the Canadian elite.* Montreal: Robin Brass Studio, 2008.

Miller, Lorne, and Ross, Neil. *One Hundred Years at the Junction Shul.* Toronto: ECW Press, 2011.

Rhinewine, Abraham, *Der Id in Kanade: fun der frantsoyzisher periode biz der moderner tsayt.* ("*The Jew in Canada: from the French period until modern times.*") Toronto: Farlag Kanade (two Yiddish volumes), 1925-1927.

Samuel, Sigmund. *In Return: the autobiography of Sigmund Samuel.* Toronto: University of Toronto Press, 1963.

Shapiro, Shmuel Mayer. *The Rise of the Toronto Jewish Community.* Toronto: Now and Then Books, 2010.

Speisman, Stephen A. *The Jews of Toronto: a history to 1937.* Toronto: McClelland and Stewart, 1979.

Stolnitz, Nathan. *On Wings of Song.* Toronto: 1968.

Troper, Harold. *The Defining Decade: identity, politics, and the Canadian Jewish community in the 1960s.* Toronto: University of Toronto Press, 2010.

Warschauer, Heinz. *The Story of Holy Blossom Temple.* Toronto, published privately, 1956.

Willinsky, Abraham Isaac. *A Doctor's Memoir.* Toronto: Macmillan Co. of Canada, 1960.

Glossary of Hebrew, Yiddish and Other Terms

ahavat Yisrael (Heb) love of the Jewish nation

aliyah (Heb., pl. *aliyot*) immigrating to Israel

amcho (??) the traditional "downtown" immigrant Jews

apikorsus, apikoros (Heb., from Greek; pl. *apikorim*) a person knowledgeable in Jewish texts who negates the rabbinic tradition and thus, according to the Mishnah, forfeits his share in the world to come. *Apikorsus*, skepticism as expressed by an *apikoros*

Aron Kodesh (Heb) the holy ark of a synagogue in which the Torah scrolls are kept

Ashkenazim, the large proportion of modern-day Jews whose ancestors settled along the Rhine from Alsace in the south to the Rhineland in the north in the early Middle Ages

baal koreh (Heb) person designated to read the Torah aloud during services in synagogue

baal tefillah (Heb) person who leads prayer service

balebosta (Yid., pl. *balebatim*) master of the house, leader of the community

bais oylom (Heb) Jewish cemetery

beth midrash (Heb) study hall; house of study

beth din (Heb) rabbinical court

Beit Hamikdash (Heb) the ancient Holy Temple in Jerusalem

bima (Heb) platform or elevated area in synagogue on which the Torah is read

bris (Heb) the ritual circumcision of Jewish boy on eighth day after birth

Chassidism (Heb., from *chesed*, acts of loving kindness) branch of Orthodox Judaism that emphasizes a joyous spirituality, promotes the performance of charitable deeds, and embraces Jewish mysticism. Founded in 18th-century Eastern Europe by Rabbi Israel Baal Shem Tov as a reaction against overly legalistic Judaism. Adherents of the Chassidic movement are called Chassidim (also Hassidism)

chazzan (Heb) cantor, singer of prayers

cheder (Heb., lit. "small room"; pl. *chederim*) a Hebrew school, often modest in size

chevra kadisha, (Heb., lit. "holy circle") burial society

chochmes (from Heb. *chochma*, wisdom) witticisms, wise sayings

chuprina [Polish-Yid] a mop of hair

daven (Yid) to pray

deutsch, deutschisher (Yid) German in outlook

drosha (Heb-Yid, pl. *droshot* or *droshes*) sermons

duchen (Heb., past tense of verb, *duchen'd, duchenen*) the act of participating in the synagogue prayer known as the Birkat Kohanim or Priestly Benediction, in which the Kohanim remove their shoes, ascend the bima (after having their hands washed by the Levi'im), cover their heads with their tallitot, and serve as the conduit for God's blessing of the congregation

Eretz Yisroel (Heb) the land of Israel, often used before the modern State of Israel came into being

folksmentsch (Yid) a person beloved by the people

frumkeit (Heb) piety

fusgeyers (Yid., lit. "foot-goers") the many impoverished Jews who left Roumania on foot in the late 19th and early 20th centuries, trekking hundreds of miles to the Austrian border, usually in order to escape persecution and emigrate to America

gabbai (Heb) person who assists in the running of a synagogue service; similar to shammes

Galicianer a Jew from Galicia or one who speaks with the Galician pronunciation of Yiddish (in contradistinction to a Litvak)

gezindikt (Yid) to be sinful, to sin

git (Heb., pl. *gittin*) decree of divorce issued by rabbinical court

goldene medinah (Yid., lit. "golden land") America, as it was commonly believed and later satirically referred to; or any other place deemed to be a "golden land"

golus (Heb) exile

g'veer (Heb-Yid., pl. *g'veerim*) a rich man

Haggadah an ancient Jewish text that sets forth the order and liturgy of the Passover Seder

Haskala (Heb) the Jewish enlightenment that began in the 18th century and marked the beginning of the wider engagement of European Jews with secular culture

halakha (Heb., adj., *halakhic*) the body of Jewish rabbinical law

hashgacha (Heb) kosher supervision.

hesped (Heb) a eulogy

heym, der heym (Yid., lit. "home," also *di alte heym*) the old country

HIAS (acronym) Hebrew Immigrant Aid Society; Canadian-based society geared to helping Jewish immigrants through all phases of their transition to life in Canada; counterpart of JIAS of America

hilfs-farband (Yid) a helping society usually set up to help relatives and other Jews in the old country

Histadrut (Heb) organization of labour unions established in Israel in 1920

hitlekh (Yid) hats

hoif (Yid) a court

Ivrit b'Ivrit (Heb., lit. "Hebrew by Hebrew") system of teaching of Hebrew through immersion, often with cultural and nationalistic rather than strictly religious overtones

JIAS (acronym) Jewish Immigrant Aid Society; see HIAS

Judenrein (German) free of Jews, as in "the Nazis sought to make Germany *Judenrein*"

kaddish (Heb) prayer that sanctifies God's name, used to separate sections of the prayer service in synagogue and repeated specifically by mourners during the period of mourning

kashrut (Heb) kosher

kehillah (Heb) community; also a local Jewish structure elected to handle community affairs. In Toronto, the *Kehillah* (capitalized) was the dispute-ridden organization elected by the community to resolve kashrut-related matters in the 1920s and 1930s

Keneder Adler (Yid., lit. "Canadian Eagle") a Yiddish newspaper published in Montreal from 1907 to 1988

kibbutz (Heb., plural *kibbutzim*) a collective agricultural settlement in Israel

klal Yisroel or *Klal Yisrael* (Heb., lit. "all of Israel") an expression meant to describe and promote a sense of shared community and destiny among all Jews

kloiz (Yid., pl. *kloizlekh*) small house of prayer; see *shtiebl*

Kol Nidrei (Heb) Aramaic declaration recited in the synagogue before the beginning of the evening Yom Kippur service nullifying vows undertaken by one's own volition

kozatzky shul (Yid) jocular term for a synagogue for Russian Jews

landsman (Yid., pl. *landsleit*) one who comes from the same town in the old country

landsmanshaft (Yid., plural *landsmanshaften*) society of Jewish immigrants from the same town or region. Sometimes a religious congregation but more often a secular organization such as a mutual benefit society. Friendship, unemployment assistance, insurance policies and burial plots were among the varied benefits of membership

Litvak a Jew from the territory of Lithuania or anyone who speaks Yiddish with a Litvak accent

machers (Yid) big-shots; the "movers and shakers" in a community

magen david (Heb) shield of David, also the Star of David that is a symbol for the Jewish people and Israel

mamzer (Yid) bastard; *mamzerel*, little bastard

mara d'atra (Heb., lit. "the master of the locality") the local rabbi who is the sole halakhic authority of the area in which he serves

Marranos (Arabic, Spanish) term, considered by some to be derogatory, for Jews living in the Iberian Peninsula (Spain) in the 15th century who converted or were forced to convert to Christianity, and continued to observe Jewish customs in secret; Anusim or crypto-Jews

mechitzah (Heb) divider in a synagogue that separates the men's and women's sections

melamed (Heb) a teacher of Hebrew and standard Jewish curriculum for school children

meshumad (Heb) an apostate

metziyes (Yid) a great and amazing bargain or an item attained as a great and amazing bargain

minhag (Heb., pl. *minhagim*) a set of customs related to observance of Jewish laws and practices, which typically vary from community to community

minyan (Heb., pl. *minyanim*) a quorum of ten adult men as required for a traditional Jewish prayer service

misheberach (Heb) a blessing of healing given during the Torah service in synagogue

misnagdim (Heb., lit. "opponents") those Jews who stood opposed to the popular Chassidic movement in the late 18th and 19th centuries

Moess Chittin (Heb., lit. "wheat money") charity given before Passover to help poor Jews afford matzah and other necessities of the holiday

Moshiyach (Heb) the Messiah, whose arrival, according to Jewish Sages, will herald humanity's entrance into a Messianic age

nachas (Yid) bursting sense of joy or pride, especially over one's children or grandchildren

niggun (Heb., pl. *niggunim*) an inspirational tune or melody, often passed down many generations and meant to enhance prayers with a special feeling of joy and inspiration

numerus clausus (Latin, "closed number") a form of bureaucratic limitation; in particular, a system of quotas or total prohibitions against the Jews in anti-Semitic realms

Pale; Pale of Settlement the only part of Imperial Russia (the western-most gubernias adjacent to Eastern Europe) in which Jews were legally permitted to reside in earlier centuries

parnosseh (Yid-Heb) one's livelihood

Peretz Shul (Yid) a Workmen's Circle secular Yiddish school named in honour of Yiddish writer Y. L. Peretz

Pesach (Heb) Passover

Peshat (Heb., lit. "simple") the most simple or straightforward reading of a Biblical or other text

Peyrek (Heb) a chapter, often of a religious text. May refer specifically to Ethics of the Fathers, whose Hebrew name, *Pirkei Avot*, is often translated as "Ethics of the Fathers" but which is literally "Chapters of the Fathers"

pilpul (Hebrew, lit. "pepper") a system of penetrating investigation into seemingly microscopic aspects of a Biblical text in order to gain a better understanding of the whole; a sort of critical and picayune hairsplitting that has drawn many detractors

rebbeim (Heb) rabbis

Sefer Torah (Heb) a Pentateuch, the Five Books of Moses in printed form

Sforim Mendele Mocher Sforim, a pioneering Yiddish writer

shammes, sexton of a synagogue

Shema (Heb) twice-daily Jewish prayer proclaiming unity of God and beginning "Hear O Israel, the Lord is God, the Lord is One"

sheneren morgen (Yid) a beautiful tomorrow

shmattah business (from Yid., lit. "rag") satirical slang term for the garment industry

shmuess (Yid) to chat or discuss

shoichet (Heb) a ritual slaughterer of permitted livestock according to the laws of *kashrut*; a kosher butcher

sholem bayit (Heb) peace at home, a valuable commodity that may require some sacrifices to maintain

shomer Shabbat, shomrei Shabbat or *Shabbos* (Heb) the practice of observing the Holy Sabbath through worship, celebrating the day and abstaining from forbidden forms of work

shtetl (Yid., plural *shtetlekh*) small town or village in Eastern Europe and Pale of Settlement where Jews lived

shtiebl (Yid., pl. *shtieblekh*) a place used for

communal Jewish prayer, usually smaller and
more casual than a formal synagogue; may be
only a business storefront or a room in a private
home

shul (Yid-German) popular term for a synagogue

siddur (Heb) a Jewish prayer-book

simcha (Heb) a joyous occasion or celebration such
as a wedding

Simchas Torah (Heb) Jewish holiday celebrating the
giving of the Torah

smicha (Heb) rabbinical ordination

T'nach (Heb. acronym) the Hebrew Bible
consisting of Torah (*Torah*), Prophets (*Nevi'im*)
and Hagiographic Writings (*Ketubim*)

tallis (Heb., pl. *tallitot*) a fringed prayer shawl

talmidim (Heb) students

TTC Toronto Transit Commission

Tehillim (Heb) the Biblical Psalms

Tehillim-Yid (Yid-Heb) a Jew who recites Tehillim

tzores (Yid) troubles, woes

UJPO United Jewish People's Order (of Toronto)

untergevorfn (Yid) thrown or tossed into

something

untergezindikt (Yid) to sin with

Vaad Hakashrut (Heb) city-based organization that
acts as the arbiter in matters of kashrut

Yamim Narayim (Heb., lit. the "days of awe") the
High Holidays

yarmulke (Heb) head covering worn by observant
Jewish men and boys

yahrzeit (Heb) the anniversary of a person's death

yichus (Heb) pedigree, ancestry

Yiddishe Gass (Yid-German) the Jewish street

yishuv (Heb) a community or settlement

yizkor (Heb) remembrance; the Hebrew prayer of
remembrance for the dead

Yom Kippur (Heb) or *Yom Ha-Din* (Heb., lit. "day
of judgement") name of solemn day of fasting,
the most holy day in the Jewish calendar; the
last of ten days of penitence beginning with
Rosh Hashanah

Yom-tov (Heb-Yid., lit. a "good day") a Jewish
holiday

Photo Credits

CITY OF TORONTO ARCHIVES Back cover, *View
northwest from Eaton factory, 1910,* f1244_it0598.
Page 15, f1244_it0523. Page 27, f1257_s1057_
it990. Page 109, f1231_it0205b. Page 134, s0372_
ss0100_it0271. Page 136, f1244_it1641. Page 140,
s0372_ss0033_it0161. Page 146, s372_s0372_
ss0032_it0039. Pages 148 & 157, f1244_it0598.
Page 160, f1244_it0341. Page 161, s0372_ss0033_
it0160. Page 166, f200_s372_ss41_it85. Page188,
f200_s 372_ss58_it1232a.

ONTARIO JEWISH ARCHIVES Page 38, item 407.
Page 42, 1977 5/8. Page 56, Dworkin, f10 item 12.
Page 57, Dunkelman fonds 39, item 14. Page 88,
1935 f92-s3-f3, f92-s3-f12. Page 123, photo 4034.

Page 141, 1996 - 9/3. Page 179, 1977 5/8.

ARCHIVES OF ONTARIO Front cover, *View from steps
of Toronto City Hall, ca 1925,* RG 2-71, COT-133.
Page 150, C301, 61; C301, 11115.

LIBRARY AND ARCHIVES CANADA Page 37,
e010800196.

Thanks to Abraham Bernstein, Adam Fuerstenberg,
Bill Gladstone, David Hart, Holy Blossom Temple,
Gurion Hyman, Sholem Langner, Rina Levi, Temi
Rosenthal, Stella Barsh Rudolph, Alice Lewis
Waldman and the Kayfetz and Speisman families
for kindly providing additional photographs.

Index

Shatz, David 48
Shemen, Nachman 56ff*, 57ff
Shiff, Murray 105
Shlisky, Yossel 136
Shopsowitz (Shopsy) 120, 123*, 131
Shtern, Sholem 64
Shulman, P. 25
Siegel, Mrs. I. H. 22
Simcoe Street Talmud Torah 23, 154
Simon, Harry 63, 96
Simpsons department store 113, 118, 183
Sinclair, Gordon 96
Singer, Joseph 62
Singer, Louis 154, 157
Singer, Rabbi Joseph 129
Slonim, Rabbi Reuben 15
Smith, Nathan 14
Smith, Stewart 86
Sokolow, Nahum 69
Solkin, Bill 105
Solomon's Delicatessen 98
Solway, Dr. L. G. 176
Spadina Avenue garment industry 45
Spadina as a Jewish area 78, 97, 123ff*, 131ff, 161
Speisman 49, 100, 137
Standard (Yiddish) Theatre 49, 53ff*, 123*, 124, 132, 173, 188*, 189*, Strand 189*
Strand Theatre (see Standard)
Steinglass, Meyer 69
Stolnitz, Cantor Nathan 74, 137
Stone, Phil 106
Strettener Rebbe (see Langner dynasty)
Sugarman, Lester 106
summer resorts 120ff
Swarbrick, Brian 134

SYNAGOGUES
Adath Israel (Anshei Roumania) 20, 28*, 46, 181
Anshei Apt 29
Anshei Chmielnik 29, 46
Anshei Drildz 30*, 32, 41
Anshei England (see Hebrew Men of England)
Anshei Kielce 30, 36*, 46

SYNAGOGUES, cont'd

Anshei Kiev 30
Anshei Lagov 30
Anshei Lida 32, 37*
Anshei Lubavitch 31*, 32
Anshei Minsk 31, 46, 125*, 126, 182
Anshei Narayev 30
Anshei New York 30, 47, 97
Anshei Ostrovtze 29, 46, 78*
Anshei S'fard (Palmerston Avenue Synagogue) 31, 40*, 182
Anshei Shidlov 29*
Anshei Slipia 30, 37*, 46, 135
Anshei Stashov 29, 46
Beach Hebrew Institute 38*
Beis Yehuda 32*
Berkeley Street Shul (see B'nai Israel Hamizrachim)
Beth Emeth 48
Beth Hamidrash Hagadol Chevrah Tehillim 15, 25, 27*, 33, 154
Beth Jacob (Poilisher Shul) 32, 41, 97, 172*, 177
Beth Jacob (Overbrook Place) 177
Beth Sholom 32
Beth Tzedec 16, 32, 194
Beth Yehuda (see Beis Yehuda)
B'nai Israel (Shaw Street) 35
B'nai Israel Hamizrachim (Berkeley Street) 35, 37-38*
Bobover Congregation 52
Bond Street Synagogue (see Holy Blossom)
Chevrah Ahavat Achim (Brotherly Love) 34
Chevrah Tehillim 11, 14, 15, 27
Chevra Shass 33, 97
Chevra Tomchei Shabbos 81
Eitz Chaim (D'Arcy Street) 35
Fellowship of Readers 34 (see also Chevrah Tehillim)
Goel Tzedec 10*, 14, 15, 25, 33, 111*, 144, 152, 154, 191, 192, 193
Hebrew Men of England (Anshei England) 25, 29, 46*, 47*, 48*, 78, 182
Henry Street Shul (see Beth Jacob)

SYNAGOGUES, cont'd

Holy Blossom 12*, 13*, 14, 15, 16*, 17*, 18*, 20, 22, 23, 26, 44ff, 47, 68, 103, 152, 192, 193
Knesseth Israel (Junction Shul) 33, 34
Londoner Shul (see Hebrew Men of England)
Lubavitch Congregation 52
Machzikei B'nai Israel 34, 40*
Machzikei HaDas (Bay Street) 152, 157*
Machzikei HaDas (North York) 34
Markham Street Shul (see Shaarei Tzedek)
McCaul Street Synagogue (see Beth Hamidrash Hagadol)
Minsker Shul (see Anshei Minsk)
Moldavian Shul 29, 46
Ostrovtzer Shul (see Anshei Ostrovtze)
Palmerston Avenue Synagogue (see Anshei S'fard)
Pirkei Kodesh (see Holy Blossom)
Poilisher Shul (see Beth Jacob)
Pride of Israel (& Sick Benefit Society) 21, 155
Shaarei Shomayim 34, 35*
Shaarei T'fillah 34
Shaarei Tzedek (Russian Shul) 34*, 41*, 42*, 43*, 181
Shearith Israel Anshei Lida (see Anshei Lida)
Shomrei Shabbos 14, 16, 17, 35, 44*, 45*, 49, 81, 153, 179*, 180*
Sons of Israel (see Holy Blossom)
Stashover Shul (see Anshei Stashov)
Tifereth Bachurim 81
Toronto Hebrew Congregation (see Holy Blossom)
Torah v'Avodah 35
University Avenue Synagogue (see Goel Tzedec)
Voice of Jacob Men of Truth 35, 36*

Thompson, Dorothy 69
Thompson, J. Laird 70
Tip Top Building 99
Toronto Gen'l Hospital 109*, 149, 163

More fine titles from NOW AND THEN BOOKS

CPSIA information can be obtained
at www.ICGtesting.com
Printed in the USA
LVOW04s2254020617
536801LV00001B/2/P